NEEDLEWORK FOR SCHOOLS

MELITA M NEAL

Nelson

Thomas Nelson and Sons Ltd
Nelson House Mayfield Road
Walton-on-Thames Surrey
KT12 5PL UK

Thomas Nelson Australia
102 Dodds Street
South Melbourne
Victoria 3205 Australia

Nelson Canada
1120 Birchmount Road
Scarborough Ontario
M1K 5G4 Canada

© Melita M. Neal 1961

First published by Blackie and Son Ltd 1961
ISBN 0-216-91078-1

This edition published by Thomas Nelson and Sons Ltd 1993

I(T)P Thomas Nelson is an International
       Thomson Publishing Company.

I(T)P is used under licence.

ISBN 0-17-438640-0
NPN 9 8 7 6 5

Printed in China

PREFACE

This book, like its companion volume *Cookery for Schools*, was written primarily for use by pupils who have examinations in mind; to be used by them as their class book for information, and to indicate the way to further study and greater appreciation of the knowledge gained. It has now been metricated and the information has been revised, expanded and brought up to date. For their generous and detailed advice in carrying out this revision, I am extremely indebted to my colleagues Dorothy Ballard and Joan Murphy.

There is a growing tendency in these times of mass production and machine skills for meticulous attention to detail in craftsmanship to be regarded as an unnecessary waste of time. In the instructions given here there is no concession to this theory and the intention is to provide clear, concise directions for the working of processes which include no extraneous or superfluous elaborations. The general principles are explained and from these the pupils can deal with a variety of instances during their future work. At the same time, contemporary methods made possible by the increasing use of automatic and semi-automatic sewing machines have been observed and recommended. New textiles have been described together with new techniques required in their use.

New sets of questions have been included, comprising some from recent examination papers and some short 'matching' questions. Acknowledgments are due to The Associated Examining Board, City and Guilds of London Institute and University of Cambridge Local Examinations Syndicate for permission to reproduce many of these examination questions. The suggestions made for further study are intended to broaden the students' conception of the craft of needlework and to lead them into private research in the wide field of subjects which contribute to the art of dress.

CONTENTS

1

EQUIPMENT

A good craftsman is known not by the number of his tools but by the efficient use of those he has. So it is with the needlewoman. A few pieces of good equipment kept in good repair and used to their greatest advantage are infinitely preferable to a large number of poorer ones badly used.

The list of items of equipment given below includes necessities as well as less essential tools, but one rule applies to all—buy the best which can be afforded and keep each piece in good condition. Tools of fine quality give more efficient service and last longer than inferior ones.

Tidy, methodical working cannot be practised too early in the development of practical skills, and the first step is to store all equipment in an orderly fashion. Some kind of container, box or basket in which to keep small tools is essential, and they should be put back in their container tidily after every use.

LARGE EQUIPMENT

In the following lists the items marked ✳ are those which are considered essential for efficient sewing. The remainder are those which add to efficiency, and often to expense, but are not absolutely necessary.

✳ Work Table

A large, smooth-surfaced table is desirable for cutting-out purposes, and it should be of a height which allows the worker to stand and sit comfortably at it. A highly polished surface is not advisable, as materials slide off easily and it gets scratched by pins and scissors.

Storage Space

Deep drawers are especially valuable for paper patterns, new material and fabric cuttings. Shallow ones should be used for threads, reserves of haberdashery and small equipment. If possible each drawer should be labelled to show its contents.

Hanging space, fitted with coat and skirt hangers, is ideal for storing half-finished garments.

If there is space available, storage can consist of a sewing-unit

1

comprising drawers, hanging cupboard and a working surface which can accommodate the sewing machine. Provision of this unit need not involve great expenditure. Plans and layouts can be found in many 'do-it-yourself' magazines.

✳ Full-length Mirror
No satisfactory fitting can be carried out unless the wearer is able to see herself and where to make necessary alterations. A mirror can be fixed to the wall or to the side or door of a hanging cupboard or wardrobe.

Dress Stand
Unless this can be made to the personal measurements of the worker (and this is not practicable for a developing figure) the model must be adjustable. Fitting is most satisfactorily carried out on the living model but a dummy is very useful for checking the hang of a sleeve, the set of a collar, the line of a seam or the position of a pocket, since the worker does not have to undress and dress again during the process.

✳ Ironing Board and Sleeve Board
An ironing board is essential for pressing garments, as is also a sleeve board. By using these boards, ironed-in creases can be avoided on the portions not in contact with the iron. Both should be covered with a pad of thick felt or blanket, or with thin foam sheeting. Easily removable outer covers should be provided in smooth, washable, lint-free, white cotton fabric.

For pressing embroidery, extra thicknesses of soft material are necessary into which the pattern may be pressed. Thin sheets of foam are excellent for this purpose, but a length of terry-towelling or a thick blanket placed under a cotton cover is equally effective.

Tailor's Ham
This is an egg-shaped pad, about 30 cm long and 20 cm wide, stuffed with wool clippings and used to press curved seams, darts and other shaped areas of garments.

✳ Iron
The iron chosen should not be too light, as the extra pressure required to obtain a good finish offsets the advantage of reduced weight. It is unlikely that anything other than an electric iron need be considered in these days, and it should therefore be heat controlled.

Steam irons are particularly useful for pressing pleats and materials best ironed slightly damp. A steam iron can of course be used dry, so there is really no necessity for two separate types of iron. Although lighter than the normal iron, a steam iron usually covers a larger area and good results can be obtained.

Irons should be kept free from dust, and flexes not allowed to twist, knot or fray.

✳ Pressing Cloth
A piece of lint-free sheeting (old and unstarched) or close-textured muslin, approximately 75 cm square, is advisable for damping and using when pressing woollens, pleats, etc.

✳ Sewing Machine
Choose a reliable make with servicing facilities. Choice of hand or electric models depends largely on the money available. Again, choose the best which can be afforded.

For care of sewing machines see p. 141.

SMALL EQUIPMENT

✳ Needles
The size and shape of the needle used depends on *a.* its purpose and *b.* the worker.

Sharps, the longer, oval-eyed needles which can be obtained in many sizes according to the material in use, are those generally used.

Betweens, which are shorter than sharps and have a bevelled eye, enable experienced workers to do very fine sewing quickly; the larger ones are used for tailoring, the finer ones for delicate fabrics.

These needles are available in sizes 1–10, the larger the number the finer the needle.

Special Needles
Darner: a long needle enabling thread to be carried from one side to another of various-sized holes and along a complete row of stitches in one operation. The eye is long in order to take wool or thick cotton thread.

Available in sizes 1–8, the smaller the number the larger the needle.

Crewel: used for embroidery. The eye is long to take embroidery threads but the length is similar to that of sharps.

Available in sizes 1–10, the smaller the number the coarser the needle.

Bodkin: a thick needle with a blunted end and long eye (or occasionally a round one) used for threading cords, ribbons, tapes, elastic, etc., through lacing-holes or hems.

Ribbon-threader: available in several forms but used for similar purposes as bodkins.

Needles should be left in their packets until required and protected against rusting. They should always be placed in a pin-cushion or threaded through a piece of material when not in use and never laid aside haphazardly.

✳ Pins

Use good quality 2·5 cm steel pins, which will not rust or mark the material. To ensure freedom from rust keep pins in a box lined with paper or a layer of woollen material which will absorb moisture. (This is the reason for the inclusion of a strip of black paper in packed boxes of pins.)

Lillikins: are fine 1·3 cm pins and are used for fixing very fine seams and hems on delicate fabrics and for holding gathering threads on thin materials, etc.

✳ Thimble

A close fit for the middle finger is necessary. A steel one is excellent; it must, however, be quite free from sharp edges which will fray sewing threads and roughen fabric surfaces.

Plastic thimbles are light and comfortable and cheaper than steel but wear through very quickly.

Silver thimbles are a joy to use, but are not hard-wearing and some, indeed, are valuable antique pieces.

Pin-cushion

A small, firmly-padded cushion for holding pins in use is helpful, particularly if attached to an elastic band worn on the left wrist.

✳ Tape-measure

Choose a strong, firm tape, clearly marked on both sides in centimetres and inches. A fibreglass tape will not fray or stretch, so there is no risk of inaccurate measurements. Keep the tape rolled when not in use and take care not to snip the edge when measuring lengths of material. Cuts, creases and pin-holes all alter the accuracy of the measurements.

Tailor's Chalk

This is a useful marker for transferring positions of notches, etc., from paper patterns to material. It can be bought in many colours; white and yellow will brush off fairly easily when used lightly.

The triangular-shaped pieces have sharpened edges which are easily blunted, but the edge can be restored with a sharp knife in much the same way as the point of a pencil.

Pieces of chalk should be kept separate from other small equipment, in a box, to avoid them being damaged.

Stiletto

A round shaft with a pointed end, mounted on a convenient handle, used for eyelet-making and for removing tacking threads. Keep free from rust and with the point protected by a small cork.

Tracing Wheel
Used with carbon paper for transferring markings from patterns to material (see p. 115). The points of these wheels are often quite sharp and are best protected with a small felt envelope. This also helps to prevent rusting.

Carbon Paper
Available in many colours. Store flat, with shiny sides of sheets folded inside. As far as possible avoid creasing.

Threads
Sylko, Trylko, Drima, pure silk, black and white sewing cotton, tacking cotton.

For thread marking use pastel-coloured tacking cotton which is easily distinguishable on the material.

For general tacking use tacking cotton.

For permanent stitching use: cotton, Sylko or Drima on cotton materials; Sylko on rayons; pure silk on silks and fine wools; Trylko or Drima on synthetics.

The colour of the thread for permanent stitching should match that of the material as closely as possible. Where an exact match is impossible the thread should be slightly darker rather than lighter.

Scissors
These should be of as good quality as possible and kept well sharpened. Avoid dropping them or using them for the wrong purposes—points may be damaged, blades forced out of alignment and screws loosened.
✳ *For general purposes*, a pair of medium-length, old scissors which will not be spoilt by cutting paper.
✳ *Small scissors* (approximately 7·5 cm blades) for snipping threads, trimming turnings, etc.
✳ *Dressmaker's shears* for cutting out; handles should be shaped for comfort in handling.
Buttonhole scissors should have a screw which can be set to ensure uniformity of length in buttonholes cut.
Embroidery scissors for fine embroidery, cutting broderie anglais motifs, etc. These should have fine, sharp points.
Pinking shears are useful for neatening edges of specimens and seams of garments to be lined, but not for any other cutting.

Metre Stick
For measuring long lengths and marking bottom hems.

Skirt Marker
A much easier method of hem-marking. A satisfactory, moderately-

priced marker in which powdered chalk is puffed in a thin line at the required position is now manufactured.

Protective Covering
It is essential to keep the work in progress clean and uncrushed, therefore as early as possible it should be hung under a cloth or plastic cover. When the work has to be carried it should be packed in a firm cardboard box or wrapped in a polythene bag.

All these precautions will be useless if the fabric is soiled by dirty hands.

QUESTIONS TO ANSWER

1 What equipment, other than a sewing machine, would you consider to be *a*. essential and *b*. not essential but desirable for the successful making of your own clothes?

2 Why is the pressing of garments important during the making up? Give as many examples as possible of the use of an iron during garment-making.

Describe the equipment you would require for efficient pressing and say how you would keep it in good condition.

3 What use would the home-dressmaker make of the following items of equipment: a pressing cloth, a tracing wheel, a stiletto, a sleeve board, a bodkin?

2

PROCESSES

STITCHES

It is essential to be able to fasten on, work, join and fasten off stitches quite mechanically, so that attention can be concentrated on the method of the process being carried out and is not distracted by the working of the stitches being used. Learn the correct way to do these stitches and form good habits of work, for this is the only foundation for the development of skill in needlework.

General rules for working stitches
 1 Choose the correct stitch for the work to be carried out.
 2 Use the correct size of needle and the right type of thread for the material.
 3 Fasten on and off securely.
 4 Wear a thimble on the middle finger of the hand which is used for sewing. This prevents the finger-tip from being rubbed sore with pushing the needle through the material.
 5 Work one stitch at a time.
 6 Never use a knot for fastening on stitches. Knots may come undone, they can tear fine materials, and they cause tiny lumps in seams or hems when the material is pressed.
 7 When threading the needle ready for sewing, it should be threaded with the end left on the reel and this end used as the shorter of the two lengths of thread. In this way the thread will be used in the same direction as that in which it has been twisted, and will be less likely to knot or fray.
 Stitches can be divided into groups, the names of the groups explaining themselves:
 1 *Temporary:* tacking (even and long-and-short); diagonal tacking; thread marking; tailor's tacks; slip basting.
 2 *Joining:* running; backstitch; oversewing; machining.
 3 *Neatening:* hemming; loopstitch; buttonholing; herringboning; overcasting; machining.
 4 *Decorative:* chain stitch; satin stitch; stem stitch; French knots; etc. (See pp. 151–3).

TEMPORARY STITCHES

As the name suggests, these stitches are removed as soon as they have served their purpose. Therefore a soft, cheap, white tacking cotton is usually used, which is much less strong than sewing cotton and will break easily if it is caught into stitching.

Even Tacking and Long-and-short Tacking
Used for holding seams and hems in position for stitching. Tacking should be worked
    a on hems: near enough to the fold to hold both turnings.
    b on seams: in such a position that stitching may be worked immediately below it.

Even Tacking

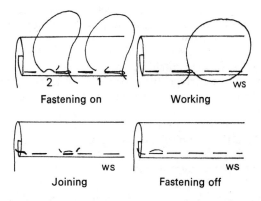

Fastening on   Working

Joining   Fastening off

Long-and-short Tacking
Worked more quickly than even tacking and particularly useful for heavier materials which it holds more firmly.

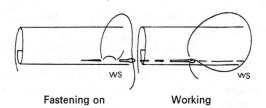

Fastening on   Working

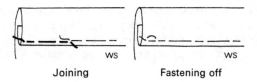

Joining   Fastening off

Diagonal Tacking

This stitch is useful for holding together two or more layers of material to prevent them from slipping out of position until they are finally fixed, e.g. collars, waistbands, pleats, linings, etc.

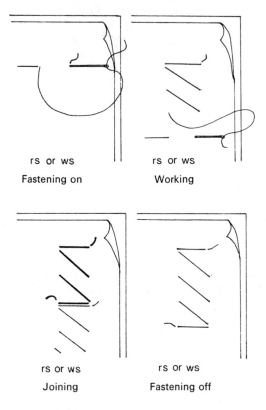

rs or ws   rs or ws

Fastening on   Working

rs or ws   rs or ws

Joining   Fastening off

Removing tacking threads: these should be removed as soon as the permanent stitching has been worked, before pressing the work. To remove quickly and easily, snip the threads at intervals and lift them out with the point of a stiletto.

Thread Marking

Used to mark fitting lines, pleat lines, etc. Worked with double thread on double material as a series of loops. The two layers of material are then pulled gently apart and the threads between cut. Lines in identical positions on both pattern pieces are thus clearly indicated. No fastening on or off is required.

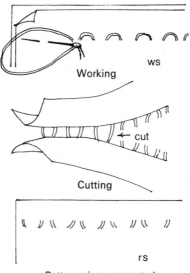

Working

ws

Cutting

← cut

Pattern piece separated

rs

Tailor's Tacks

Used for marking positions of notches, darts and other important details shown on printed and perforated paper patterns. When using patterns with a considerable number of dots or perforations (for seam lines, darts, tucks, and button-holes on a blouse, for example) it is a good idea to work each set of perforations in a different colour of thread to avoid confusion.

ws

Working

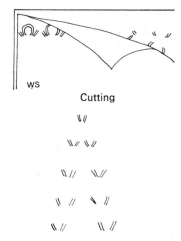

ws

Cutting

A dart marked in tailor's tacks

Slip Basting

This is a tacking stitch worked from the right side of the fabric and used to hold two pieces of material together and match a pattern exactly, e.g. in matching stripes, either straight or in chevrons. The needle takes up a small piece of the under section and comes out inside the fold of the upper one. For final stitching the two right sides are placed together and the stitching worked exactly over the basting. As this may cause difficulty in removing the tacking thread it is advisable to use a matching thread for the purpose.

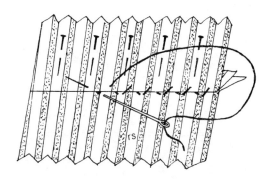

JOINING STITCHES

Used for joining two or more separate pieces of material together. The thread used should match the type of material as far as possible: e.g. cotton, Sylko or Drima on cotton; Sylko or Drima on rayon; Trylko or Drima on synthetics; pure silk on silk. Woollens and other heavy materials may be stitched with silk, Sylko or Drima.

Running Stitch
Worked from right to left, one stitch at a time.

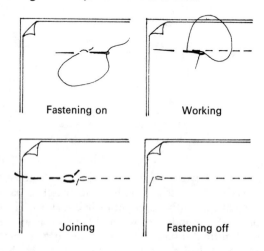

Fastening on   Working

Joining   Fastening off

Backstitch
Worked from right to left. If one side of the stitch will be more easily visible than the other it should be worked from the visible side.

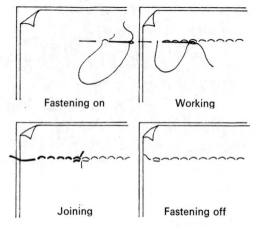

Fastening on   Working

Joining   Fastening off

Oversewing

Used to join two folded edges or selvedges together (e.g. ends of deep hems, attaching tapes, etc.). Worked from right to left, with the edges being joined held away from the worker.

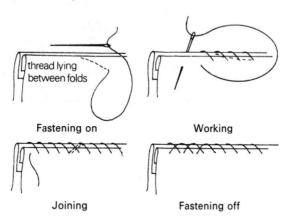

thread lying
between folds

Fastening on   Working

Joining   Fastening off

Machining

A section on machine-stitching begins on p. 141, but it is essential to know now how to recognize a correct machine-stitch and how to fasten off ends.

Note: 'Stretch stitch', 'flexi-stitch' and 'elastic straight stitch' are all terms for similar stitches.

top tension too tight   top tension too loose

Correct stitching   Incorrect stitching

R.S. — — — — — —   ————————   — — — — — —

W.S — — — — — —   — — — — — —   ————————

Correct   Top tension   Top tension
tension   too tight   too loose

Fastening Off Machine-stitching

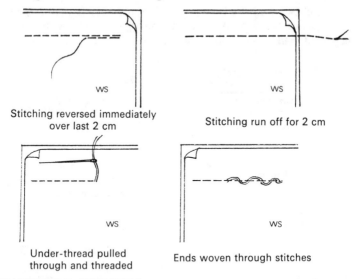

Stitching reversed immediately
over last 2 cm

Stitching run off for 2 cm

Under-thread pulled
through and threaded

Ends woven through stitches

NEATENING STITCHES

These are used for securing hems and turnings, and for preventing raw
edges from fraying. Threads matching the material should be used.

Hemming

Worked from right to left with the hem held over the fingers of the left
hand and the rest of the garment held towards the worker.

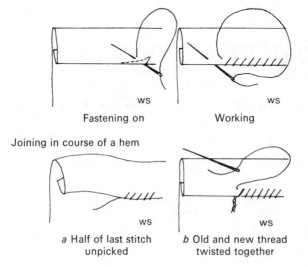

Fastening on

Working

Joining in course of a hem

a Half of last stitch
unpicked

b Old and new thread
twisted together

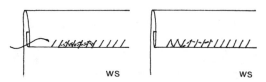

c Twisted ends tucked under   Fastening off

Invisible Hemming

This stitch is used for fixing hems on lightweight skirts and is invisible when completed. It is a looser stitch than ordinary hemming and does not fasten down the folded edge of the hem; it therefore does not make an obvious hemline on the right side. The hem is fixed with tacking well above the folded edge, which is rolled backwards as the stitch is worked, or the whole hem may be folded back as shown. This stitch may also be used to fix a bound hem on heavy skirts.

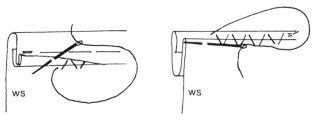

Loopstitch

Worked over raw edges, from left to right, with the edge held towards the worker, and is often wrongly referred to as 'blanket stitch'. It is also used to neaten raw edges of seams inside garments (e.g., flat seam, see p. 24, overlaid seam, see p. 28).

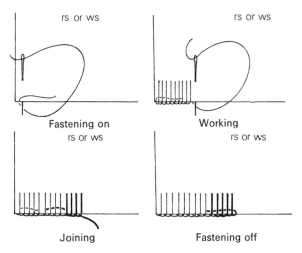

Buttonholing

Worked over raw edges, usually double, from left to right with the edge held away from the worker.

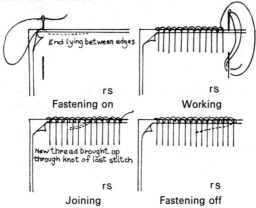

Herringboning

Worked from left to right over single turnings with the folded edge held away from the worker.

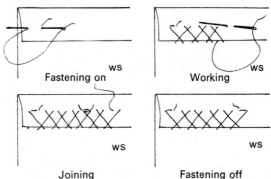

Overcasting

Worked from left to right and suitable for working over raw edges (e.g. the edge of a flat seam, see p. 24) which may or may not be first strengthened with a line of machine-stitches.

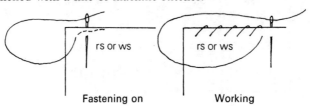

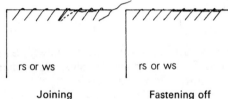

Joining	Fastening off

Machining

These machine-finishes are the equivalent of overcasting and loopstitch.

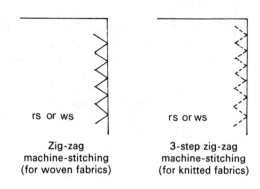

Zig-zag machine-stitching (for woven fabrics)	3-step zig-zag machine-stitching (for knitted fabrics)

Gathering

This stitch does not fit easily into any of the groups mentioned, but it is one which will almost certainly be needed in the process of making garments.

It may be worked by hand or with the machine adjusted for a long stitch (see p. 71). At least two rows should be worked, one exactly below the other, the lower one on the stitching line and the upper one just below the edge of the seam allowance. Both lines of stitches are pulled up together to the required length and fastened off. Gathering threads cannot be joined.

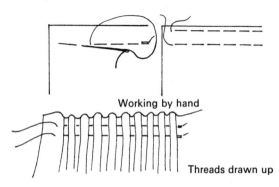

Working by hand

Threads drawn up

FURTHER STUDY

THINGS TO DO

1 Make specimens of all the stitches shown, using two different colours of thread for the purpose of showing joining. Use double material for temporary and joining stitches, and hems or turnings on single material for the neatening stitches.

2 Make a simple design worked in the decorative stitches shown in Chapter 4 and suggest where it could be used.

QUESTIONS TO ANSWER

1 Complete the following statements by filling in the blank spaces with words taken from the right-hand column.

a .... stitches are those which will be removed once their purpose has been served.	right to left
b Markings used to indicate pleat lines and fitting lines until stitching is completed may be made in chalk but to avoid the danger of these being rubbed off they are better worked as	tailor's tacks
	left to right
c In order to ensure that darts, tucks, pockets and other style features are evenly balanced they are marked through double fabric with	temporary
	Drima
d A thread specifically manufactured for stitching synthetic fabrics is called	left to right
e .... is a frequently used sewing thread which is made from cotton.	3-step zig-zag
f Oversewing is a joining stitch used to fasten two non-fraying edges together and worked from	Sylko
g Loopstitch is a neatening stitch worked over a raw edge (or edges) from	zig-zag
h Overcasting is a neatening stitch, sometimes worked over a line of machine-stitching, and worked from	thread marking
i Woven fabrics can be neatened by using a .... stitch worked by machine.	
j When knitted fabrics are neatened by machine a .... stitch is used.	

2 Describe with diagrams the working of the following stitches and give an example of the use of each one:

a tailor's tacking

b basting

c gathering stitch

d edge stitching

e overcasting.

3 Give three types of tacking which you would use in preparing a garment for its first fitting. How does each one assist the worker? Illustrate your answer with diagrams and give detailed instructions for working each type of tacking.

4 Describe with the aid of diagrams the working of four of the following stitches and give examples of their use:

a invisible hemming

b loopstitch

c herringbone

d slip basting

e overcasting

f buttonhole stitch.

SEAMS

Seams are used for fastening together two or more layers of material neatly and securely. The choice of seam depends on:

a the material being used (e.g. a French seam is ideal for the side seams of a nylon slip but quite unsuitable for the seams of a tweed skirt)

b the garment being made (e.g. a double-stitched seam is suitable for jeans but not for a cotton dress)

c the position of the seam (e.g. a French seam is used successfully for the side seams of slips but is not suitable for attaching the midriff section to the upper bodice)

d the shape of the seam (e.g. a French seam is quite suitable for the straight side seams of blouses but is not so easily worked on the curved seams sometimes required for attaching yokes).

General rules for working seams

1 Threads used must be suitable for the material.

2 The width of the seam depends on the texture of the material. Generally speaking, the finer the material the narrower the seam should be. This will, however, depend on whether the material frays easily, or is particularly loosely woven.

3 All seams of the same type on a garment must be of similar widths.

4 The strength of the seam will depend on the firmness or otherwise of the stitching. Hand-worked stitches must be frequent and regular and those worked by machine must be of a suitable tension and length for the material. (This must be tested on a *double* piece of the same material first.)

5 To avoid puckering of seams on very delicate fabrics it is

advisable to place a piece of tissue paper behind the layers of material before stitching them.

FRENCH SEAM

This seam is very useful for underwear, blouses, children's dresses and most straight seams on thin materials. No raw edges are visible when the seam is complete and there is no stitching which shows on the right side of the work.

When completed the seam should be pressed towards the back of the garment.

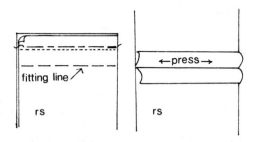

1 Place raw edges together, wrong sides facing.
Tack and stitch 6 mm outside the fitting line.
2 Remove tacking. Press seam open and trim turnings to 4 mm.

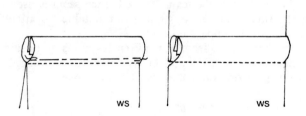

3 Fold along stitched line with right sides together, carefully working out the stitching between the fingers.

Tack 6 mm from edge, enclosing raw edges completely.

Stitch immediately below tacking line (i.e. on line of seam allowance).

4 Remove tacking. Press seam towards the back of garment.

Faults which may occur

1 Raw edges or frayed threads showing on the right side.

2 'Pockets' along the outer edge of the seam on the wrong side.

3 Dragging or puckering of the material on the underside of the seam.

How to avoid them

    1 Trim raw edges with sharp scissors after the first stitching and make sure that the second line completely encloses them. This can be checked by holding the seam to the light after working the second tacking.

    2 Press the turnings completely open and flat after working the first stitching.

    3 Work the seam out very carefully and examine *both* sides to see that there are no pleats and that the fitting lines match.

DOUBLE-STITCHED SEAM

The principle of this seam (sometimes called 'machine-felled') is similar to that of a run-and-fell seam. It is, however, worked entirely by machine from the right side of the garment.

    This seam is very suitable for thick lingerie materials as well as for finer ones, particularly in the making of pyjamas and panties, where a curved seam is required.

    A good average turning allowance for this seam is 1·3 cm.

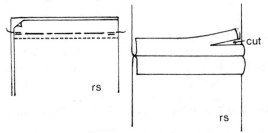

    1 Place raw edges together, wrong sides facing.

    Tack and stitch 1·3 cm from edges (or on line of seam allowance).

    2 Remove tackings. Press seam open.

    Cut down back turning by half of its depth.

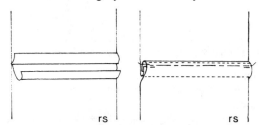

    3 Make 5 mm turning on front free edge.

    4 Turn fold towards back of garment, tucking raw edge underneath that of back turning.

    Tack. Stitch close to edge. Remove tacking.

Faults which may occur

    1 Seam turned towards front of garment.

    2 Frayed edges appearing after second line of machining has been worked.

    3 Fullness or puckering on the wrong side between the two lines of stitching.

    4 Variation in the width of the seam.

How to avoid them

    1 Make certain that it is the back turning which is cut down after the first stitching.

    2 Turn under sufficient of front turning to be firmly caught by second line of machining, and work this as close as possible to the edge of the fold.

    3 Press turnings open after the first stitching and tack firmly before working the second machining. Examine the back of the seam carefully before stitching.

    4 Cut edge of garment evenly and sew along the line of seam allowance.

IMITATION OVERLOCK-STITCH SEAM

This stitch can be produced on some fully automatic swing-needle machines (e.g. Viking, Pfaff and Singer) and is the domestic machine method which is the nearest equivalent to industrial overlocking. It is suitable for fine jersey fabrics and for transparent materials on which it replaces the French seam. The stitch is referred to as 'stretch' or 'elastic' (on Viking machines) and as 'flexi' (on Singer machines).

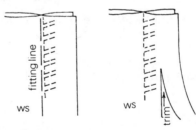

ELASTIC STITCH SEAM

This is a machine-made backstitch which is particularly suitable for jersey and other stretch fabrics, for setting in sleeves and for crutch seams in trousers.

Faults which may occur in either of the above
    1 Fraying of the fabric after stitching and/or trimming.
    2 Puckering.
How to avoid them
    1 Set the machine to make the stitches closer together or the bight (width of stitch) wider.
    2 Check tension carefully and make sure that the needle is sharp.

CROSSED SEAMS

In the fork of pyjamas or panties without gussets, one double-stitched seam crosses another at right-angles. Care must be taken that
    a meeting portions of seams turn to the same direction
    b a continuous seam line is formed.

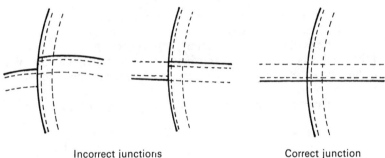

    Incorrect junctions   Correct junction

How to avoid seam-junction faults
    1 Work leg seams separately, turning each to back of leg.
    2 Tack leg portions together, beginning tacking at junction and working from there to top of back body-seam and again from junction to top of front body-seam. Machine in continuous line from centre front to centre back, easing machine-foot over double thickness at junction. Allow generous turning on seam.
    3 Cut down left-hand portion of seam turning.
    4 Turn under raw edge of right-hand portion and tack from junction in each direction as before.
    5 Machine in continuous line from centre front to centre back, easing foot again over junction and making sure that stitches are as close as possible to the edge of the fold.

FLAT, PLAIN OR DRESSMAKER'S SEAM

This is a favourite seam in garment-making, suitable for almost any outer garment in most materials. No stitching is visible on the right side, the strength of the seam depending upon one row of machining worked along the seam allowance line. Therefore the depth of turning is important and should vary from 1·3 to 2·5 cm according to:

    a the texture of the material

    b the fraying qualities of the material

    c the method of neatening planned.

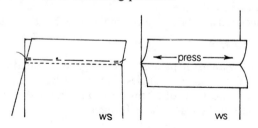

1 Place raw edges together, right sides facing.

Tack and stitch along line of seam allowance.

2 Press open, using a pressing cloth on heavy materials.

If the turning is likely to mark the right side of the material place a piece of thick paper or thin cardboard between the garment and the turning before pressing.

3 Neaten raw edges by one of the following methods:

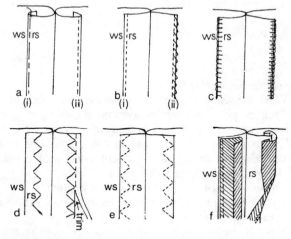

    a Edges turned under and (*i*) tacked, (*ii*) machined. Suitable for lightweight dress materials.

    b Raw edges (*i*) machined and (*ii*) overcast. Suitable for heavier dress materials.

    c Raw edges loopstitched (over line of machining or not according to texture of material). Suitable for heavy materials which do not fray easily.

d Edges neatened with one line of machine zig-zag stitch and trimmed closely. Suitable for dress and skirt-weight materials.

e Edges neatened with 3-step zig-zag stitching. Suitable for preventing edges of jersey and bonded fabrics from rolling and also for easily frayed fabrics which will not accept ordinary zig-zag stitch.

f Edges bound with crossway strip (of a finer material). Suitable for unlined coats and jackets.

Faults which may occur

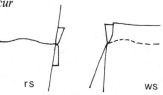

1 Waviness in the seam line on the right side caused by badly matched fitting lines.

2 Edges of turnings leaving an impression on the right side after pressing.

3 Turnings not lying flat on the wrong side, making seam pull right side of garment out of shape, caused by curving of seam line.

4 Stripes or grain in material not meeting accurately.

How to avoid them

1 Measure turning carefully if seam allowance is not clear and tack seam at an equal distance from the raw edges along its entire length. Machine immediately below the tacking line in a smooth, unbroken line.

2 Use paper or thin cardboard between turnings and garment when pressing.

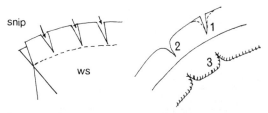

3 Before pressing seam open, snip turnings diagonally. Curve corners of snipped edges slightly and overcast to neaten.

4 Tack very carefully, watching both sides of turning with each stitch taken.

B

Pinking

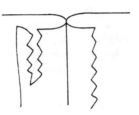

It is often suggested that the edges of these seams should be pinked, using pinking shears. This is not, however, recommended as a suitable method, the short-cut threads of the points being easily frayed away by wear or washing. There is, however, no reason why these seams should not be treated in this way on garments which are to be lined and will be dry-cleaned rather than laundered.

WELT SEAM

This is a decorative seam used on outer garments made in medium or heavy-weight fabrics.
Method

1 ⎫
2 ⎭ as for flat seam (see p. 24).

3 Press turnings to one side along the line of seam allowance.

4 From R.S. work a line of machine top-stitching through both turnings, the required distance from the seam line.

Note: The seam allowance should have been increased 1·3 cm beyond the line of top stitching.

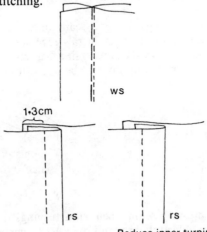

Reduce inner turning
on bulky fabrics

5 Neaten raw edges as for overlaid seam (see p. 27).

OVERLAID SEAM

This is a most useful seam for undergarments and many outer ones. It is a strong seam providing that adequate turnings are allowed.

    1 The first stitching, joining two portions of the garment, is worked on the seam line, from the right side.

    2 The raw edges are neatened according to the texture.

Method

    1 Turn the edge of the portion to be overlaid to the wrong side for the depth of the seam allowance. (If this is turned from the right side a good, straight fold line is more easily obtained than when turned from the wrong side.)

    If a curved line is required, the edge must be snipped at intervals before being turned.

    Tack on the edge of the fold.

Straight edges

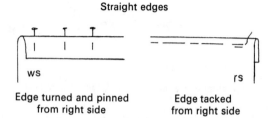

Edge turned and pinned   Edge tacked
from right side   from right side

Curved edges

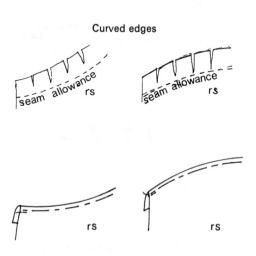

2 Place the tacked edge to the seam line of the under portion of the garment, right sides uppermost, and tack into position.

Straight edge tacked into   Curved edge tacked into
position over under portion   position over under portion

3 Edge-stitch by machine or secure with imitation hem-stitching. (See Chapter 4, p. 154). The latter method gives a very attractive finish for lingerie seams.

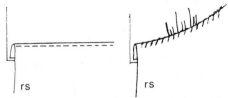

Edge stitched by machine   Edge secured with
                              imitation hem-stitching

4 Neaten raw edges by one of the following methods:

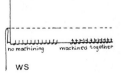

a Raw edges loopstitched: suitable for lingerie and for heavier materials; also for straight or curved seams

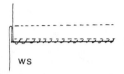

b Raw edges machined together, trimmed and overcast: suitable for heavier materials, straight and curved seams

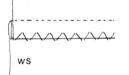

c Raw edges neatened with machine zig-zag stitch

Decorative Variations of Edge-stitched Overlaid Seam

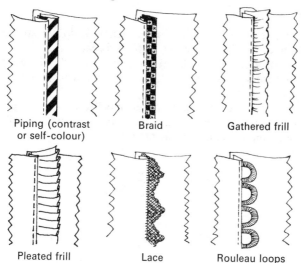

Piping (contrast or self-colour)

Braid

Gathered frill

Pleated frill

Lace

Rouleau loops

TUCKED SEAM

This is particularly suitable for heavy skirts, dresses, etc. The depth of the tuck depends on the width of the seam allowance on the overlaid portion. This turning should be twice the width of the finished tuck + seam allowance. The under portion has the normal seam allowance.

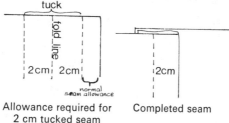

Allowance required for
2 cm tucked seam

Completed seam

Neaten raw edges by methods *a*, *b* or *c* as for overlaid seam, or one of the following:

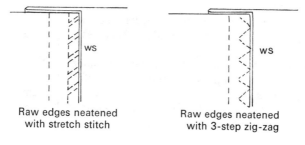

Raw edges neatened
with stretch stitch

Raw edges neatened
with 3-step zig-zag

FURTHER STUDY

THINGS TO DO

1 Work specimens of *a.* French seam, *b.* double-stitched seam, *c.* flat seam, *d.* overlaid seam and *e.* tucked seam.

Choose a suitable material for each one and, where alternative methods of neatening are possible, show small portions of each method on the same specimen.

2 Prepare folders of stout paper, labelled clearly on the outside. Mount the specimen on the inside and, opposite it, write brief notes on suitable uses, materials and garments for each one.

 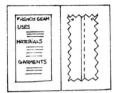

Suggested folder

3 Collect pictures from magazines and catalogues of garments on which these seams would be used. Make use of these for reference and for illustrating the folders prepared.

QUESTIONS TO ANSWER

1 Complete the following statements by filling in the blank spaces with words taken from the right-hand column.

a A .... seam is a strong, neat seam which is particularly suitable for underwear and pyjamas.

b The best seam to use on fine fabrics which fray easily is a .... seam.

c A seam which may be used on either under or outer garments and which may be made decorative by inserting piping or other trimming between the two layers is called a .... seam.

d If the turning is made wider and the stitching worked well in from the edge it becomes a .... seam.

e The most commonly used seam for outer wear is a .... seam as no stitching is visible from the right side.

f The raw edges of a flat seam on an unlined jacket should be neatened with ....

right

loopstitching

wrong

double-stitched

dressmaker's

binding

French

right

tucked

g The raw edges of an overlaid seam on a medium-weight loosely-woven fabric may be neatened with .... | overlaid

h The first line of stitching in a French seam is worked on the .... side of the garment.

i The first line of stitching worked when making a welt seam is made on the .... side.

j The first line of stitching in a double stitched seam is worked on the .... side.

2*a* Name *three* conspicuous seams used to create style interest.

b Sketch *three* garments which will illustrate the use of each seam.

c Describe and illustrate the method for preparing, stitching and neatening *one* of the examples. (A.E.B.)

3*a* Name *five* seam finishes in general use today, giving an example of each and in each case naming the garment fabric.

b Illustrate how one hand-sewn finish is worked. (A.E.B.)

4 A different seam is required for making up each of the following:

a a brushed-nylon nightdress

b a woollen tweed suit.

Name the seams you would use. Describe and illustrate how each is worked. (A.E.B.)

5 Suggest, with diagrams, quick, neat and suitable seam and hem finishes for each of the following:

a a cotton dress

b a rayon brocade dress

c a wool jersey dress

d a child's dress in terylene. (C & G)

FASTENINGS

Fastenings of garments should have as long a life as the garments they serve, providing that they are chosen and attached correctly.

Fastenings chosen should be suitable for:

a the garment (zip fasteners in skirts, buttons and buttonholes in pyjamas)

b the material (loops and buttons for fraying materials, buttonholes and buttons for firmer ones)

c the position (buttons and loops where edges meet, buttons and buttonholes where they overlap)

d the age of the wearer (ribbons for babies' garments, 'Velcro' for children's garments).

Whatever the fastening chosen the method of attaching should comply with the following rules:

1 Fastenings should always be sewn on to double material.

2 They should be as inconspicuous as possible unless used as decoration.

3 If the garment is likely to be washed, fastenings should also be washable (e.g. covered buttons should have washable, rustless moulds).

TAPES AND RIBBONS

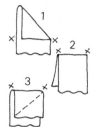

Preparation

Turn the end of the tape over as a square of itself:

1 Turn raw edge to selvedge edge.

2 Crease across tape (*x* to *x*).

3 Turn back diagonal fold.

Attaching

1 Place edge of turning to edge of garment and pin in position.

2 Hem round three inner edges, one stitch across each corner. Do not fasten off thread.

3 Turn tape back level with the edge of garment and oversew edges together.

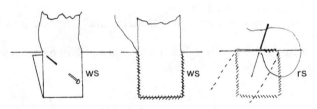

Method for overlapping edges

1 Prepare ends as before.

2 Attach tape to wrong side of overlap as shown above.

3 Place tape with raw edge downwards on required position on underwrap. Pin in position.

4 Backstitch close to edge all round the square.

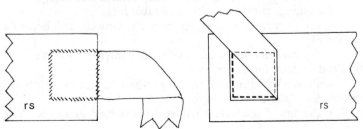

Finishing free ends of tapes
1 Make a narrow hem on wrong side of free ends.
2 Hem turning down and oversew ends.

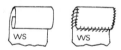

Finishing free ends of ribbons
Cut to shape. Do not hem.

PRESS FASTENERS

Press fasteners consist of two parts, one with a flattened base supporting a knob, the other a thicker section deep enough to provide a hole into which the knob fits.

Method of attachment
1 The knobbed portion, having a flat base which will make no impression when the material behind is pressed, is sewn on to the wrong side of the overwrap.
2 The thicker part with the hole is sewn to the right side of the underwrap.
3 Fastening on and off should be worked as a double stitch just under the edge of the fastener.
4 Buttonhole or oversewing stitches may be used, both serving their purpose efficiently, but buttonholing is stronger.
5 Whichever stitch is used the same number should be worked in each hole, the actual number of stitches depending upon the size of the fastener.

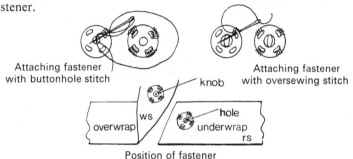

Attaching fastener with buttonhole stitch

Attaching fastener with oversewing stitch

Position of fastener

HOOKS AND EYES

Hooks

The hook portion of the fastening is always stitched to the wrong side of the overwrap, with the edge of the hook in line with the edge of the garment.

Attaching

    1 Secure the hook to the edge of the garment with two stitches under the hook.

    2 Anchor the shaft of the hook just above the loops with two stitches across it.

    3 Buttonhole round the loops.

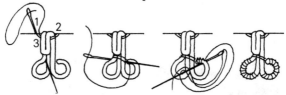

Eyes

There are three types of eyes for completing the hook fastening:

    a metal loops (suitable for use on openings in which edges meet and do not overlap)

    b metal bars (suitable for openings in which the edges overlap)

    c worked bars (suitable for the same uses as metal bars and also for use on meeting edges).

Metal Loops

The loop is sewn to the wrong side of the edge of the garment opposite the hook. Sufficient of the loop should extend over the edge to allow the hook to fasten into it.

Attaching

    1 Two anchoring stitches are worked over the edge of the garment at each side to hold the loop fast.

    2 Buttonhole stitches are worked round the loops as for the hook.

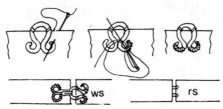

Completed fastening

Metal Bars

Bars are sewn to the right side of the underwrap. No anchoring stitches are required, the loops being buttonholed into position.

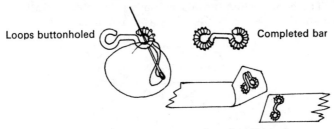

Loops buttonholed   Completed bar

Completed fastening

Worked Bars

These may be used in place of metal bars when a more inconspicuous fastening is required. The strands are worked in thread matching the garment and are then buttonholed.

On overlapped fastenings the bar should lie almost straight on the material but if used on meeting edges the strands may be long enough to form a shallow loop.

Working

1 Thread is fastened on with a small double-stitch and a straight stitch is made across the material. A small portion of the cloth is picked up and the thread is taken back to the other end of the stitch.

2 This is repeated as many times as is necessary for the size of the hook being used.

3 The strands are buttonholed.

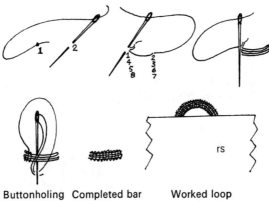

Buttonholing   Completed bar   Worked loop
over strands

'VELCRO' FASTENING

This is the touch-and-close nylon fastening which can be purchased in small lengths.

The hook section (firm layer) should be attached to the upper wrap and the looped section (soft layer) to the under wrap.

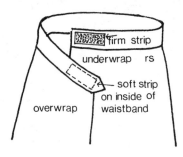

BUTTONS

Buttons must be provided with a shank to allow movement of the loop or buttonhole between the button and the garment. (A shank is a stem between the button and the material, and without this the button will not stay fastened.)

Some buttons are made with shanks or with loops.

If they have no shanks of their own, stems of thread must be made as the buttons are sewn on.

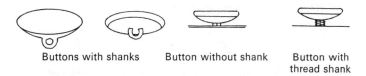

Buttons with shanks   Button without shank   Button with thread shank

Buttons without Shanks or Loops

1 Fasten on thread at required position of button.

2 Place centre of button over fastened-on thread, bring thread through first hole in button to right side of button.

3 Place across the button a pin, a bodkin, a matchstick or a knitting needle, according to the length of shank required. (The thicker the material, the longer the shank required; the longer the shank the thicker the pin/needle necessary.)

4 Pass thread across pin and through second hole, to back of material. Repeat this as often as is necessary for the size of the button, keeping the stitches on the wrong side lying one over the other.

5 Remove pin, bring needle out between button and material and pull button to the end of the long stitches formed.

6 Wind the thread 3 or 4 times round the stem of stitches formed and take the needle through to the back of the material.

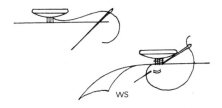

7 Buttonhole over the stitches at the back of the material and fasten off.

If double material is not available on which to sew the button, place a smaller button at the back of the material and make stitches to pass through holes in both buttons.

Buttons with Shanks or Loops

Stitch on these buttons in the same way as 2-holed buttons but

      a omit pin or needle across button

      b pass needle sideways through hole instead of up and down.

Buttons with Four Holes

    1 Sew these on in the same way as 2-holed buttons, but make back stitches lie in two rows. Neaten these stitches separately.

    2 Threads over top of buttons may be arranged in any of the following directions, but they must all be alike in any series of buttons.

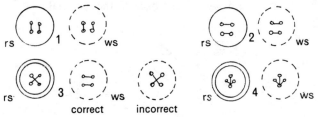

Position of Buttons

Buttons should be sewn on at least half their diameter in from the edge of the garment

Faults in sewing on buttons

    1 Too close to the edge of the garment.

    2 No uniformity in the direction of stitches in a series.

    3 No shank.

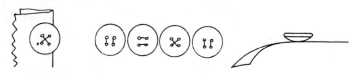

Worked loops for buttons

Worked loops are suitable for fastening buttons when the edges of the opening meet, e.g. back neck opening; and sometimes when they overlap, e.g. at corner of overlap under collar.

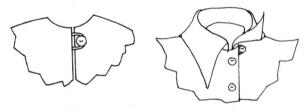

1 Place a piece of thin card behind the required position of the loop and place pins in position as shown.

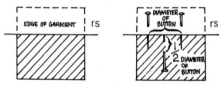

2 Fasten on thread with a double stitch at one pin and work strands back and forth from pin 1 to pin 3, passing thread round pin 2 and finishing at pin 3.

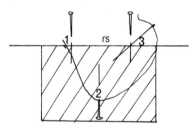

Repeat stranding as often as size of loop requires.

3 Remove card, turn loop round and work buttonhole stitches over the strands.

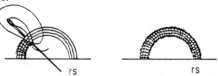

Note: A similar method on a small scale and with the strands lying flat on the material gives a worked bar as used with a hook.

A similar method on a larger scale, also with the threads straight, gives a carrier for a belt.

Flat Rouleau Loops

A rouleau loop is more decorative than a worked loop and is particularly effective when several are worked side by side and used with covered buttons.

A similar method makes a decorative edging for neck edges of dresses.

1 Cut a crossway strip of the required length for loop + 2·5 cm and at least 5 cm wide. (If narrower, the strip is more difficult to manage.)

If several loops are required the strip may be cut long enough for all the loops (e.g. one loop may require 2·5 cm, therefore strip would be cut 5 cm long to allow for turnings; therefore six loops of this size would require a strip 30 cm long.

(For cutting of crossway strip see p. 51)

2 Fold strip in half lengthways, right sides facing, and tack along the middle.

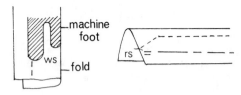

3 Machine along the length of the strip, with the outer edge of the small portion of the foot against the fold.

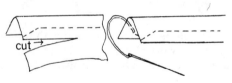

4 Cut down the turning to just under the width of the stitched tube and attach a double thread to one thickness of the material.

5 Pass the needle, eye foremost, through the tube.

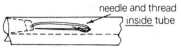

needle and thread
inside tube

6 Pull the tube inside out, remove the thread.

7 Mark the width and depth of the required loop on the raw edge of the garment (right side).

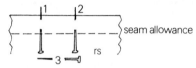

seam allowance

rs

8 Arrange the loop between the pins (1 and 2), with the seam of the loop uppermost. Tack along the line of the seam allowance.

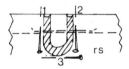

rs

9 Place right side of facing to right side of garment, raw edges together. Tack and machine along line of seam allowance.

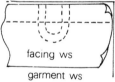

facing ws

garment ws

10 Remove tackings, trim turnings and turn facing to the wrong side of the garment. Tack and edge-stitch the turned edge, from the right side.

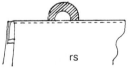

rs

11 On wrong side, turn under raw edge of facing and edge-stitch.

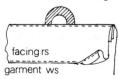

facing rs

garment ws

Worked Buttonholes

Cutting: buttonholes should be cut straight to a thread, in the same direction as the strain of the fastening (horizontally on cuffs, waistbands, pyjama coats, etc.; vertically on blouse fronts).

Length: the length of the buttonhole should equal the diameter of the button + 3 mm.

Position: the buttonhole should begin at least half the diameter of the button from the edge of the garment.

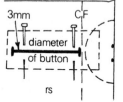

Buttonhole position marked with an oblong of tacking worked round position to hold fabric edges together

Note: If buttonhole scissors are used, test the size on paper or an odd scrap of material before cutting the buttonholes on the garment.

Amount of thread required: a 2·5 cm buttonhole requires 1 metre.

Type of thread: on fine materials the thread used may be the same as that with which the garment is stitched.

Working

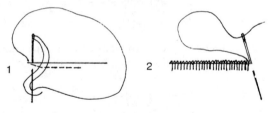

·1 Thread passed between the two layers of material and needle in position for first stitch.

2 First side completed and needle in position for first stitch of round end.

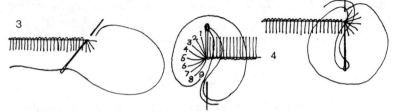

3 Oversewing stitches worked at the round end, there being no room for the knots of buttonhole stitches. There should be 5, 7 or 9 stitches, the middle one being in line with the buttonhole.

4 Last oversewing stitch of round end and first buttonhole stitch of second side worked together.

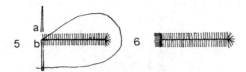

5 Take thread from knot of last stitch to other end of stitch, and then from a to b (i.e. unknotted end of stitch at each side). Repeat this once and bring out needle at point 1.

6 Work buttonhole stitches at right angles to those along the sides, making the knots lie along the strands previously made. There should be the same number of stitches as at the round end, the middle one in line with the buttonhole.

Note: The round end of the buttonhole should be at the end nearer to the garment edge. It is at this end that the shank of the button will rest, so it must not be crowded with knots of buttonhole stitches. The square end is to prevent the end of the buttonhole from splitting with use.

On garments on which the buttonholes are cut vertically, they may be worked with either two round or two square ends, the latter giving the smarter effect.

Bound Buttonholes

This method is suitable for all but transparent and very bulky materials. It can be used on most outer garments.

1 Cut a crossway strip the length of the buttonhole required + 5 cm, and 5 cm wide.

Mark the line of the buttonhole with small tacking stitches.

2 Place the right side of the strip to the right side of the garment, the line of tacking lying over the buttonhole line on the garment.

Tack through both thicknesses of material, along the line of small tacking stitches.

3 Starting at the centre of one long side, work a rectangle of machine-stitches, the length of the required buttonhole and twice the finished depth of the bindings. Overlap the first three stitches to finish off.

Note: The number of stitches along both long sides and across both ends must match.

4 Snip at centre of bindings to within 6 mm of the stitches and mitre the corners as shown.

5 Turn crossway strip to wrong side and bind the turnings evenly across the opening. Tack into position and overcast the bindings together. Press lightly on the wrong side.

6 On the wrong side oversew the small pleats together (made at each end of the binding strip). Trim the ends to 6 mm.

7 Turn facing back to wrong side and tack around buttonhole. Mark the position of the buttonhole through to the facing with a pin at each corner.

Snip buttonhole on facing as in binding (see step 4).

8 Turn under the cut edges of the facing and hem them to the binding, making sure that stitches do not go through to the right side of the garment.

Remove tackings and press.

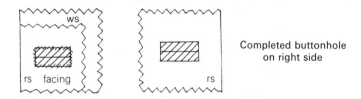

Completed buttonhole on right side

Machine-made Buttonholes

These are suitable for use on all light- and medium-weight materials as a quick finish, particularly on materials which fray easily, and can be worked on any swing-needle sewing machine. The buttonhole is cut *after* working, which is an obvious advantage to a beginner who is tackling difficult materials.

The method of working varies with the make of the machine (semi- and fully-automatic models), so for step-by-step instructions reference should be made to the booklet supplied with the machine.

ZIP FASTENERS

The fastener should always be chosen bearing in mind the garment as well as the colour of the material for which it is to be used. One or two well-known firms of fastener manufacturers produce various weights of fasteners in different coloured packings, for everything from slips to boots. The study of advertisements is useful for detailed knowledge of these, but most haberdashery retailers will give advice on choice.

Fitting a zip fastener into a seam I

This is a neat and simple method of inserting a fastener into the seams of such garments as skirts, dresses, shorts, etc.

1 Press the seam open and continue the neatening of the edges of the seam right to the top of the opening.

Tack along the pressed edges of the opening, from the right side.

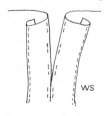

2 Tack in zip fastener with the edge of the teeth to the edge of the opening. This is most easily worked by keeping the fastener closed at first and tacking up 1 cm from the bottom of the tape at one side, opening it while tacking the remainder of the side. Repeat this process on the second side. The top of the fastener should be in line with the seam allowance line of the skirt waist.

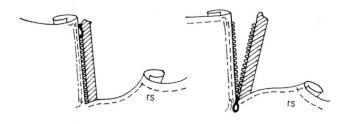

3 Machine from the right side 6 mm from the edge of the opening, starting at the top of the fastening, working a line of stitches at right angles across the bottom and continuing stitching up the second side. This is most easily worked on the machine by using a single-sided zipper or cording foot 6 mm from the edge of the stitching.
Note: Do not let the zipper-foot come into contact with the teeth of the fastener.

4 On the inside, hem the bottom edges of the fastener tape to the seam turning.

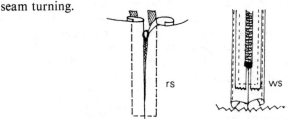

Fitting a zip fastener into a seam II
A

1 Finish the edges of the seam for its full length, according to the material.

2 Turn back the right-hand side of the opening along the fitting line and tack. Repeat on the left-hand side, with the fold 3 mm outside the fitting line.

3 Place the folded edge of the right-hand side of the opening to the teeth of the right-hand side of the fastener. The top of the fastener should be in line with the seam allowance line of a skirt waist and 6 mm below that of a neck edge. Tack and stitch into position by hand, using backstitch, or by machine, using the zipper or cording foot.

4 Tack the left-hand side of the opening to the zip tape so that the folded edge of the opening just covers the stitching on the opposite edge.

Stitch by hand, using back stitch, or by machine, using the zipper or cording foot, 6 mm from the fold. Work a diagonal line of stitching across the bottom of the fastener.

5 Catch the bottom of the fastener tape to the turning.

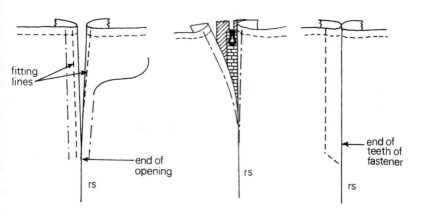

or B

1 Place the right side of the fastener (closed) to the right side of the right-hand side of the opening, with the inner edge of the left-hand tape to the fitting line.

Tack and stitch as above.

2 Turn fastener to right side and tack along the stitched fold.

3 Proceed as for left-hand side of opening as shown in A.

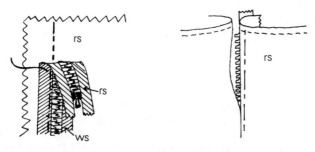

Note: When a zip fastener is inserted into the back or front seam of a dress, tunic or blouse, the neck edge should be finished and the opening completed with a hook and loop.

Zip fasteners in side openings of dresses
Insert by one of the methods described above but work a squared line of stitching across both ends.

FURTHER STUDY

THINGS TO DO

1 Work specimens of fastenings described in the preceding section.

2 Prepare folders as described in the previous section, showing these specimens together with particulars of garments and positions suitable for their use.

3 Collect advertisements by well-known manufacturers of fastenings. Add prices and become familiar with names and costs.

4 Find as many examples as you can of the types of fastenings used on historical garments. Make sketches of these. Show their development into modern methods of fastening.

5 Make a collection of as many different types of buttons as you can.

QUESTIONS TO ANSWER

1 Complete the following statements by filling in the blanks with words taken from the right-hand column.

a Loops for use with buttons can be made with thread or	oversewing
b The knobbed part of a press fastener is stitched to the .... of an opening on the .... side.	vertical
c 'Eyes' for use with metal hooks are stitched to the .... side of the	buttonholing
d Room is made for a button to be slipped through a buttonhole by providing it with a	horizontal
e Buttonholes are worked on the .... of an opening.	right
f Unless made by machine, or bound, a buttonhole must be finished with .... stitch.	overwrap
	underwrap

g The round end of a buttonhole is worked in .... stitch.	rouleaux
h On a collar band or a cuff the buttonhole would be cut in a .... direction.	wrong
i On this type of buttonhole the .... end is at the end nearer the outer edge of the portion of the garment.	overwrap
	round
j Down the front of a loosely fitting garment the buttonholes may be cut in a .... direction because there is no strain on the fastening.	shank

2 Give detailed instructions for the insertion of a long zip fastener into the back seam of a woollen dress. Illustrate your answer with diagrams.

3 Suggest five different fastenings which could be used on dresses and explain why each would be chosen and where it would be used. Illustrate your answer as fully as possible.

4*a* What points would you consider when choosing a zip fastener for the back opening of a white cotton piqué tennis dress?

b Using clearly-labelled diagrams and brief notes explain how you would:

(*i*) prepare the back opening

(*ii*) insert the zip fastener

(*iii*) neaten the top of the zip with the neck facing of the dress.

(C.U.B.)

5*a* Name *two* different ways of making button loops, sketching an example of each in use on garments.

b Describe and illustrate the making of *one* method in detail.

(A.E.B.)

6 Describe, with the aid of diagrams, the making of a bound buttonhole.   (A.E.B.)

7 Give points to be considered when buying a zip for each of the following:

a a woollen skirt

b the centre back of a fine crêpe dress with no waist seam

c a pair of denim jeans

d the front opening of an anorak.   (A.E.B.)

8 Describe, with the aid of sketches, how to make a rouleau. Suggest a way of using it decoratively *a.* on heavy material and *b.* on lightweight material.   (C & G)

CUTTING AND JOINING ON THE CROSS

The value of strips of material which have been cut on the cross is that they will stretch and also ease round curves. On a larger scale, bodices and skirts cut in this way will drape well and cling to the figure, moulding themselves to shape much more effectively than will straight-cut pieces. *Note:* Care must be taken when handling cross-cut materials to avoid distortion. Fabric cut on the cross for design effects only, e.g. checks or stripes, should be supported with a straight-cut interfacing.

THE STRUCTURE OF MATERIAL

Material is woven by threading weft threads alternately over and under warp or selvedge threads.

The warp threads are stretched tightly on looms in this process and will not stretch further after the material is woven.

The weft threads are not stretched during weaving and will therefore 'give' slightly when the material is pulled. They do not stretch appreciably, however, and cannot easily be worked round curved edges.

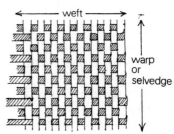

Much enlarged weave

From the above facts a test for finding the direction of the warp or selvedge threads may be evolved. On a perfectly square, raw-edged piece of good quality material the direction of the selvedge threads may be determined by pulling each straight edge firmly.

The warp threads will not 'give'.

The weft threads *will* 'give'.

A second test is to pull the material sharply in each direction.

The warp threads emit a sharp crack.

The weft threads emit a duller sound.

Diagram of direction of true cross and bias lying across straight warp and weft threads

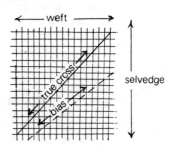

The warp and weft threads are firm and will not stretch. If a line is drawn across them so that each right angle is cut in half, the cut edges will stretch considerably.

Compare these threads with the wooden slats forming garden trellis-work. If the slats are tacked together in squares, forming right angles, the edges remain rigid. If formed into diamonds, however, the lattice will expand and contract as required.

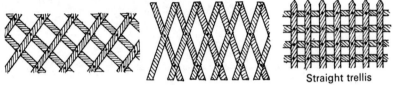

Lattice trellis

Straight trellis

The *bias* is off the true straight but is not true to the cross. It will therefore stretch more than straight-cut material but not nearly so generously or as regularly as cross-cut fabric.

Commercial 'bias' binding bought by the yard is actually cut on the true cross.

CUTTING CROSSWAY STRIPS

Crossway strips used for neatening and decorating garments are usually cut from the irregularly shaped pieces left over after cutting out the garment sections. With experience, the direction of threads in irregularly shaped cuttings can be recognized, but less experienced workers are advised to work only with square-cornered pieces.

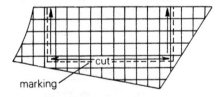

Marking rectangle from irregularly shaped piece of material

1 Fold over one corner of the material so that the weft edge lies along the selvedge threads. (Notice position of right angles.)

2 Mark line of fold with pins and open out the flap.

3 Using a ruler or guide, mark with pins or chalk lines parallel to the fold line, the distance between them being the required width of the strips. Cut along the marked lines.

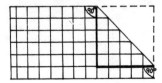

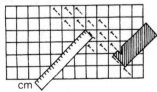

JOINING CROSSWAY STRIPS

1 Lay out the strips side by side, right sides, uppermost.

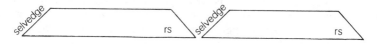

2 Cut the ends parallel to the selvedge edges.

3 Place the selvedge edges together, right sides facing, corners overlapping for the depth of the seam.

4 Tack and stitch on the seam line between the angles formed by the overlapping corners, as indicated above.

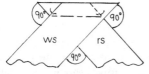 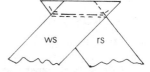

5 Remove tacking and press turning out flat.

6 Snip off the protruding corners.

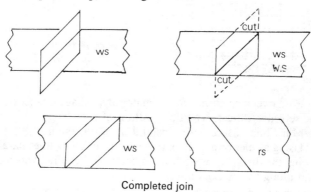

Completed join

Faults which may occur

1 Join making an uneven level in the completed strip. This is caused by placing the edges of the pieces together for joining without overlapping the turning.

2 Stripes running in opposite directions. This is caused by confusing the right and wrong sides of woven material and thus joining a weft edge to a selvedge one.

3 Similarly, the grain of materials with an irregular weave may run in different directions. Reason as above.

4 Joins running in different directions instead of parallel to each other. This is caused by not cutting the ends of each strip parallel to each other before joining.

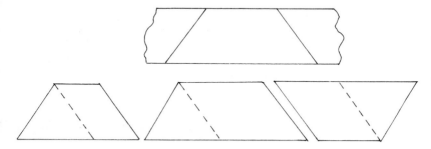

THE USE OF CROSSWAY STRIPS

Crossway strips are used for:

    a binding raw edges
    b facing raw edges
    c bound buttonholes (see p. 43)
    d rouleau loops (see p. 40)
    e pipings

Binding Raw Edges

Bindings serve two purposes: they may be used for decoration and for neatening or, of course, both at once.

Decoration: the binding material used is visible on both sides of the garment and attractive effects may be achieved by using crossway strips which contrast with the garment in texture or colour, e.g. striped bindings on plain material, satin on wool, etc.

Neatening: binding is a useful neatening for the edges of armhole seams. It is not always suitable to use strips of the garment material for neatening seams and a softer material may be used for this purpose instead, e.g. hems of a thick woollen dress may be bound with matching rayon lining or those of a linen dress may be finished with mercerized cambric commercial bias binding.

Method

    1 Cut a crossway strip twice the required finished width plus twice the turning allowance wide and as long as is necessary.

    2 Place the right side of the strip to the right side of the garment, raw edges together. Tack and stitch the required finished width from the edges. Stretch the strip slightly while tacking it on. If the edges form a concave curve, stretch the edge of the strip slightly as it is tacked on. On convex curves, ease it slightly.

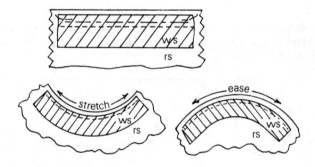

    3 Make a narrow turning to the wrong side on the free edge of the binding strip.

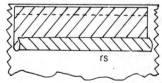

4 Fold the turned edge over the raw edges to the wrong side of the garment, tack just above the machining and hem into position. Be very careful not to let the hemming stitches go through to the right side, particularly on thin materials.

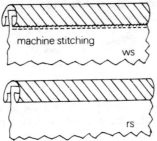

Facing Raw Edges
Crossway strips may be used as facings for neatening hem lines, armholes, collar and cuff joins, etc.

Method for straight edges
1 Place the right side of the facing strip to the right side of the garment, raw edges together. Tack and stitch 6 mm from the edge.
2 Turn up facing strip along stitched line and tack into position.
3 Turn under narrow turning on free edge. Tack to garment, making sure that the facing is lying quite flat against the garment. Slip hem into position.

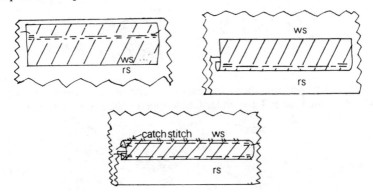

Method for curves

1 Place the right side of the facing strip to the right side of the garment, raw edges together. Tack and stitch 6 mm from the raw edges.

2 Snip turnings diagonally, also the lower edge of the facing. The diagonal snips allow the turnings to overlap inside convex turnings and spread inside concave ones.

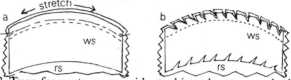

3 Turn facing to wrong side, tacking along seamed edge. Make a narrow turning on the free edge of the facing and tack it *a*. leaving it unattached to the garment, *b*. to the garment.

4 Edge-stitch the outer edge of the faced edge from the right side. On the inner edge *a*. edge-stitch facing and hem it to the seam, leaving the rest free, *b*. slip hem it to the garment.

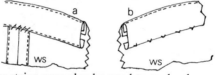

Crossway strips may also be used to make decorative edges.

Working

1 Place right side of facing strip to wrong side of garment, tack and stitch 6 mm from the edge.

2 Snip turnings diagonally, on both edges.

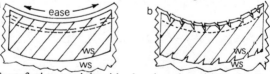

3 Turn facing to right side, leaving the width of a thread of the facing strip showing above the garment edge on the wrong side. Tack along seamed edge. Turn under free snipped edge and tack to garment.

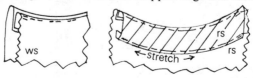

4 Edge-stitch both edges of facing. (Edge-stitching along the outer edge prevents the garment material from rolling over to the right side.)

Pipings

Pipings can be used to decorate edges and seams. They may be made to include a soft cord if a firmer, bulkier effect is required, but care should be taken to shrink the cord before use on garments which may require frequent washing. Piping cord is made from cotton and it is possible that the cord will shrink when the covering material does not, causing a puckered effect.

Contrast (in texture or colour or pattern) may be introduced to give added decoration, e.g. satin on wool, white on colours, stripes on plain material.

Piped collar and cuffs for blouses and dresses

Piped seam for skirts and dresses

Piped roll collar for jackets and dressing gowns

Method without cord

1 Cut a crossway strip the necessary length and twice the desired width plus twice the seam allowance.

2 Fold it in half lengthwise, wrong sides together, and press along the folded edge. Tack.

3 Place the raw edges of the folded strip to the edge of one section of material, right sides facing. Tack along seam line.

4 Tack the second section over the strip, raw edges together and right sides facing. Tack along seam line. Stitch over tackings.

5 Turn two sections with wrong sides together and piping outwards. Tack and edge-stitch into position.

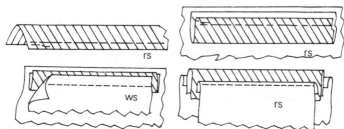

c

Method with cord

1 Cut crossway strip and place piping cord inside the fold. Tack close to the cord.

2 Proceed as for method without cord, but use the piping foot on the machine in order to work stitching as close to cord as possible.

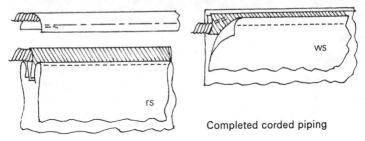

Completed corded piping

FURTHER STUDY

THINGS TO DO

1 Work specimens of crossway joins on *a*. plain material, *b*. striped material, *c*. textured material. Include one incorrect join in each material.

2 Work specimens of binding, straight and crossway facings, and piping. Show facings on right and wrong sides.

3 Prepare folders of *a*. crossway strip joins, *b*. bindings and *c*. facings. Include particulars of uses of each.

4 Find illustrations of garments in which crossway strips are used as neatenings or decoration. Mount these and indicate the use of the strip.

QUESTIONS TO ANSWER

1 Complete the following statements by filling in the blanks with words taken from the right-hand column.

a When cross-cut strips are joined the stitching should be worked along the .... threads.	binding
b The first step in preparing the strips for joining is to cut the ends .... to each other.	wrong
c When selvedge threads are folded to lie along the weft ones the true cross is the direction of the .... formed.	selvedge
d Any other cross direction is known as the	piping
e A .... is a cross-cut strip folded in half lengthwise and inserted into a seam.	right
	overlaid

f A .... is a cross-cut strip enclosing a raw edge.

g A .... is a strip neatening a raw edge and visible only on one side of the garment.

h A binding strip is attached first to the .... side of the garment.

i When a strip is to be used as a decorative facing it is stitched first to the .... side of the garment.

j A piping can be inserted into a flat or an .... seam.

bias

diagonal

facing

parallel

2 Describe with the aid of diagrams how to cut and join cross-way strips. Give, with illustrations, as many ways as possible of using these strips.

3 Describe in detail how to finish the armholes of a wild silk sleeveless dress with a narrow bind. (C & G)

4 Why is material which is 'cut on the cross' used so frequently in dressmaking? Sketch *three* examples of its varied use. (C & G)

FACINGS

Facings may be worked on the right or wrong side of the garment and, like bindings, may be used as decoration and neatening.

Decorative effects may be achieved by using

a contrasts in texture

b contrasts in colour

c shaped inner edges of facings.

On straight edges the facing should be cut as a straight strip.

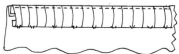

On gentle curves the facing should be cut on the cross.

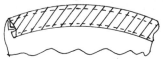

On deep curves and other shaped edges the facing should be cut to the same shape as the edge to be faced.

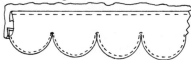

For crossway strips used as facings, see p. 55.

CUTTING SHAPED FACINGS

Although the example is for the square neck of a dress, the principle is the same for any other shaped facings required, e.g. round neck facings, sleeve facings, shaped hem facings, etc.

1 Fold front and back portions of the bodice in half lengthwise and pin together round neck edges and armholes. Place folded edges to the edge of a sheet of paper.

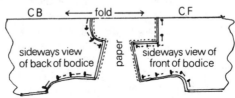

2 Draw round neck edges and along shoulder seams. Remove bodice portions.

3 Measure from the neck edges the required depth of facing, plus 1·3 cm turnings, and mark the shape with pencil. Add 1·3 cm turnings to the shoulder seam line if shoulders of garment have already been joined. Cut out paper pattern.

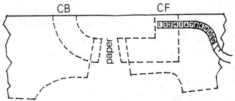

4 Place pattern on double facing material (right sides together), centre front and centre back to fold. Pin in position and cut out.

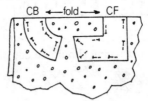

Attachment of facing

1 Place shoulder seams of facing sections together, right sides together. Tack and stitch on fitting line. Press turnings flat and trim to 6 mm.

2 Join shoulder seams of bodice if necessary, using exactly the same turning for the join as in the facing.

3 Place right side of facing to right side of bodice, neck edges

together. Make sure the shoulder seams lie one over the other. Tack and stitch in position all round neck edge, making sharp angles at front corners.

4 Snip corners to stitching line and at intervals along curved neck edge.

5 Turn facing to wrong side, tack along neck edge. Make turning along free edge, making the last turn along straight lower edge of front facing. Curved edge of back facing must be snipped. Edge-stitch neck edge and lower edge. Catch facing to shoulder seams.

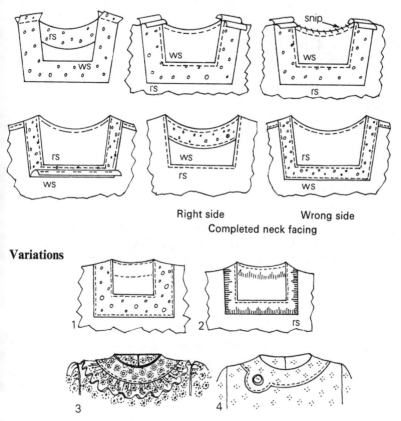

Right side   Wrong side
Completed neck facing

Variations

1 Facing worked on right side. Worked in similar method to above but with right side of facing to wrong side of garment, and lower edge stitched to the garment.

2 Facing turned to right side and caught down with a decorative stitch.

3 Frill placed between facing edge and garment.

4 Shaped facing.

ADAPTED FACING

This is a useful finish for sleeve and pocket edges.

1 Place right side of facing to right side of garment, raw edges together. Tack and stitch on stitching line.

2 Turn facing to wrong side of garment leaving 3 mm of facing showing on right side. Tack in position.

3 Edge-stitch on right side of facing.

4 On inside, neaten free edge of facing and catch to seams.

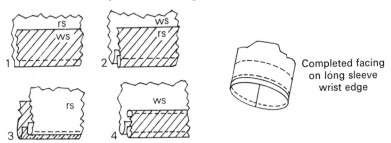

Completed facing
on long sleeve
wrist edge

FURTHER STUDY

THINGS TO DO

1 Work specimens of *a*. shaped facings showing as many variations as possible, *b*. an adapted facing, *c*. a faced hem.

2 Prepare folders of *a*. shaped facings and *b*. straight facings, including particulars of their use on various garments.

QUESTIONS TO ANSWER

1 You have a pattern for a dress with a collar but you have decided to make the collar detachable. Describe and illustrate how you would finish the neck edges of the dress and the collar. (A.E.B.)

2 Give instructions for making the pattern of the neck facing for a blouse which has a scoop neckline. Describe how to make up the facing and how to apply it. Illustrate your answer with diagrams. (A.E.B.)

OPENINGS

The style of opening chosen should be suitable for:

    a the garment

    b the material

    c the position of the opening.

The type of fastening required must also be considered when choosing the opening.

The four most useful types of opening are:

a the continuous wrap opening
b the faced opening
c the box-pleat opening
d the fly-front opening.

The continuous wrap opening may be adapted for use on very thin materials and undergarments; the faced, box-pleat and fly-front openings may be worked to have decorative effects.

All openings should be cut straight to a thread wherever possible; exceptions must be made when the opening is a continuation of a seam.

CONTINUOUS WRAP OPENING

This is suitable for the wrist openings of long sleeves and for the back openings of children's garments.

It may be fastened with hooks and bars, or press fasteners.

Preparation

Cut a strip of the garment material twice the length of the opening and 5–7·5 cm wide, as appropriate for the garment. The direction of the selvedge of the strip should match that of the garment.

Working

1 Pull apart the edges of the opening so that they lie in a straight line.

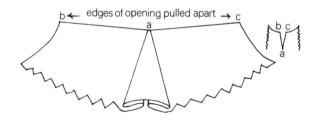

2 Place the right side of the strip to the right side of the opening, raw edges together.

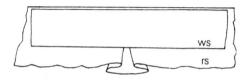

3 Tack and stitch 6 mm from raw edge. The turning on the wrong side of the garment will decrease in width towards the end of the opening (i) but will remain the same width from the beginning to the end of the strip.

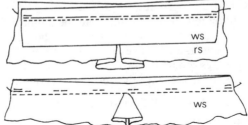

4 Make 6 mm turning on free edge of strip and fold it over the raw edges of the opening. Tack turned edge just above the first stitching and hem into position. (As in working a binding, no stitches must show on the right side.)

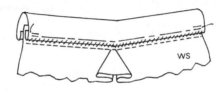

5 Fold the front part of the opening back along the stitching line, place over the back portion and press.

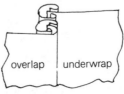

FACED OPENING

This type of opening is suitable for front and back neck openings and wrist openings of long sleeves set into a band.

It can be made decorative by:

a turning the facing to the right side

b working machine-stitched rows on the right side

c using contrasting facing on the right side

d shaping outer edge of facing on the right side.

The fastening used is similar to that for bound openings: link buttons, button and loop, hook and eye; or, as previously mentioned, a zip fastener.

Preparation

1 Mark the position and required length of opening on the garment with a line of tacking stitches. This should be as straight to a thread as possible.

2 Cut facing section the length of the opening + 5 cm, and a proportional width, e.g. 15 cm long and 5 cm wide, 20 cm long and 10 cm wide. Mark the opening as on the garment.

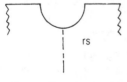

Preparation of garment

Preparation of facing

Working

1 Place the right side of the facing to the right side of the garment, with tacking lines lying one over the other.

Place pins through the tacking lines to find correct position and tack through both thicknesses of material along previous tacking line.

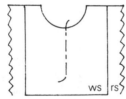

2 Machine or backstitch 6 mm from top of marked opening towards point, sloping stitching inwards. Continue from point to 6 mm from top at other side. Make sure that a true V-shape is stitched and that no curves are formed.

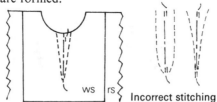

Incorrect stitching

3 Cut down line of tacking between stitches, snipping carefully right into the point.

cut

4 Turn facing to wrong side and tack folded edge. Edge-stitch from the right side. Great care must be taken at the point of the slit to make a firm, strong turn.

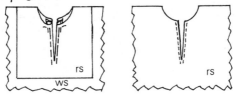

5 On the wrong side of the facing make a turning on each side and along the bottom edge. Tack and edge-stitch from the right side.

Variations

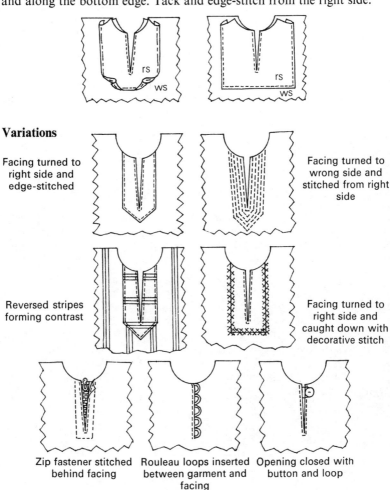

Facing turned to right side and edge-stitched

Facing turned to wrong side and stitched from right side

Reversed stripes forming contrast

Facing turned to right side and caught down with decorative stitch

Zip fastener stitched behind facing

Rouleau loops inserted between garment and facing

Opening closed with button and loop

BOX-PLEAT OPENING

This opening is a neat, decorative finish for a blouse or shirt-waister style dress. (See sketch p. 77).

Preparation

Requirements: *a* Pattern (front bodice pattern with separate facing.)
 b Fabric (self or contrast)

Cutting the facing (R.H. front only, L.H. front remains an ordinary wrap opening):   Width = required box pleat + 2 × turning.
 Length = length of bodice pattern piece.

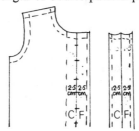

Working

 1 Tack and stitch right side of facing to wrong side of garment along neck edge from C.F. and down front edge. Clip neck turning at C.F. Trim and layer the turnings.

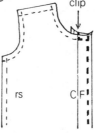

 2 Turn facing to right side, work out the seam edges, tack and edge-stitch.

 3 Turn under free edge of facing and edge-stitch.

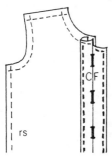

Note: On tab openings such as this buttonholes should always be cut vertically

FLY FRONT OPENING

(Instructions for adaptation from ordinary wrapover)

1 Place bodice pattern onto extra pattern paper, turning under front turning or facing.

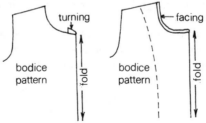

2 Plan extension of pattern. Note that 'button stand' refers to concealed double panel through which the buttons are inserted.

Finished depth of fly front = existing button stand × 2, e.g.

Button stand 1·9 cm: Fly front 1·9 × 2 = 3·8 cm

Button stand 2·5 cm: Fly front 2·5 × 2 = 5·0 cm

a Mark spots beyond front bodice edge three times width of fly front + one turning, e.g.

3·8 cm+3·8 cm+3·8 cm+1 turning

5·0 cm+5·0 cm+5·0 cm+1 turning

b Draw in lines parallel to front edge.

c Mark top, inner and lower fold.

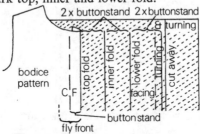

3 Fold as shown and trim neck edge.

Note that it is important to mark all fold lines and the neck edge very carefully.

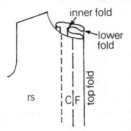

4 Fold facing and fly front back towards right side of garment along inner fold line.

5 From C.F. stitch along neck edge to lower fold line. Stitch down this line for 1·3 cm and then continue, parallel to neck edge, to inner fold. Neaten free edge of facing according to fabric. Machine-tack down lower fold line as shown (i.e. stitch with longest possible stitch).

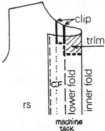

6 Clip neck edge at C.F. and lower fold line as shown in f. Trim remainder of neck edge.

7 Turn facing and fly front back towards wrong side along line of machine tacking and press.

8 Remove tacking and work vertical buttonholes through lower layer.

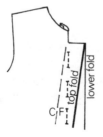

9 Catch the two folds together between each buttonhole with a small worked bar.

10 Top-stitch through all the thicknesses of fabric at the width of the finished fly front from the folded edge.

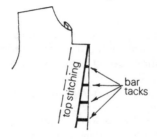

FURTHER STUDY

THINGS TO DO

1 Work specimens of box-pleat, fly front, faced and continuous wrap openings.

2 Prepare folders of these openings and particulars of their use and suitable fastenings for each.

QUESTIONS TO ANSWER

1 What points have to be taken into consideration when deciding which type of opening to use on a garment? Suggest two different openings which could be used at the back neck of a blouse. Give detailed instructions for working *one* of these.

2*a* Many commercial patterns give the use of a faced opening at the wrist for long sleeves. Suggest an alternative method for a wrist opening on a garment made from a cotton/polyester fabric.

b Explain briefly and illustrate how the opening should be worked. (A.E.B.)

METHODS OF CONTROLLING FULLNESS

1 Gathering
2 Darts
3 Tucks
4 Pleats
5 Easing

Fullness is already allowed in commercial patterns:

a to accommodate the curves of the figure

b to provide decoration.

GATHERING

Gathering is one of the most useful and easily worked methods of reducing fullness. (See p. 17.)

It is particularly suitable for soft and fine fabrics and may be used for skirts, sleeves, frills and fullness set into yokes, etc.

Allow up to twice the width of material for gathering as is required for finished width.

Wherever gathers are worked they must be set into fitted portions of garments (e.g. gathered bodice into midriff), or 'stayed' with a straight piece of fabric behind the gathered portion.

At least two rows of gathering should be worked, one just outside the stitching line and one 6 mm further away. This 'sets' the gathers and makes neatening of the raw edges easier and more reliable. Long lengths of gathers are best worked in several short sections to facilitate pulling up without danger of breaking threads. If a gauged or ruched effect is required, several rows of gathers are worked below the stitching line and all pulled up together to the required tension.

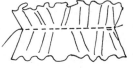 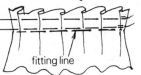 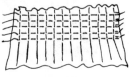

| Untidy edge gathered with one row of stitches | Neat effect of edge gathered with two rows of stitches | Ruching |

Working gathers by hand

    1 Fasten on with a double stitch.

    2 Work stitches by passing thread over twice the amount of material as is picked up. Stitches in each row should lie one above the other.

    3 Pull up both threads together and wind them round a pin until gathers are evenly distributed at the required tension. Fasten off each thread securely.

Working gathers by machine

    1 Thread the machine in the usual way.

    2 Adjust the stitch to its longest length.

    3 Work two rows of stitching as by hand.

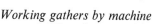

    4 Fasten off beginning of each thread.

    5 Draw up underthread of both rows of gathering together and fasten off both threads.

    To make sure that gathers are evenly distributed, the middle of the gathered edge and of the fitted portion should be marked before gathers are worked. These must be placed together for joining. On long lengths, quarters and even eighths may be marked on both edges.

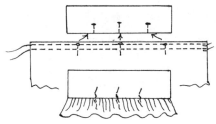

After gathers are joined to the fitted portion of the garment the raw edges should be neatened as for overlaid seams. (See p. 28).

Setting Gathers into Bands
(e.g. sleeve edge into wristband).
Method showing no stitching on right side
    1 Gather edge of sleeve according to instructions above.
    2 Close sleeve-band seam.

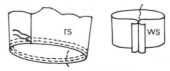

Attachment
    1 Place right side of band to right side of sleeve edge, with seams and middle markings matching. Tack along inner row of gathers from gathered side.
    2 Stitch along tacked line from gathered side.
    3 Turn seam allowance on free edge of band to wrong side. Fold band to wrong side of sleeve and tack turned edge just above stitching.
    4 Hem into position, making sure that stitches do not go through to right side.

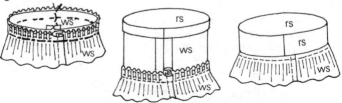

Method showing stitching on right side
    1 Prepare sleeve edge and band as for method above.
    2 Work as for previous method, through steps 1, 2 and 3, *but* place the right side of the band to the *wrong* side of the sleeve. Tack and stitch along lower row of gathers.

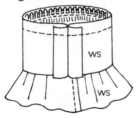

3 Turn under free edge of band and fold to right side of sleeve. Tack and stitch turned edge just below first row of stitching. Edge-stitch outer edge of band to correspond with inner one.

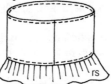

Further rows of stitching worked at equal distances are effective.

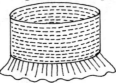

Shaped cuffs may be attached to sleeve edges by the same method, whether with or without openings.

DARTS

Darts give a smooth, moulded line to garments and if properly worked are quite inconspicuous. They are actually small pleats tapered towards the fuller part of the figure from a narrower part:

 a back neck darts (to accommodate nape shaping)

 b front and back shoulder darts (to accommodate bust and shoulder bone)

 c underarm darts (to accommodate bust shaping)

 d elbow darts in long or three-quarter length sleeves

 e skirt darts (to accommodate hip shaping)

 f waist darts. (These may be tapered at both ends if bust and hip fullness is to be accommodated with no join at waist.)

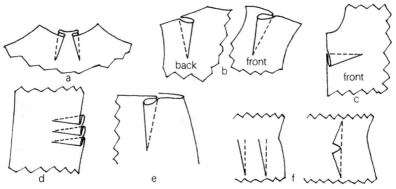

Working

    1 For recognition and marking of darts from garment pattern see pp. 108–15.

    2 Tack darts as indicated and stitch from wide end to point. Fasten off ends.

    Make sure that the stitching line is perfectly straight and that stitching ends on the very edge of the fold, otherwise the dart will bulge on the right side.

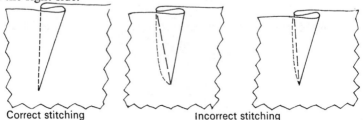

Correct stitching   Incorrect stitching

    3 Press darts towards centre front or back of garment to give the appearance of being turned outwards from the right side.

    4 If material is bulky, cut down the fold of the dart and press out flat. Neaten edges.

    5 On transparent or thin materials the dart may be stitched and neatened with stretch stitch (on swing-needle machine); or as a tapered French seam.

trim

ws

6 Darts may be tapered at both ends. In order that these may cause no dragging on the right side of the garment, the dart should be snipped across its widest part to allow it to 'spread'. The edges should then be neatened with loopstitching or buttonholing.

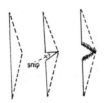

Note: A French dart is a shaped dart curving from the side seam at waist level to the point of the bust, incorporating the usual underarm and waist darts into one.

TUCKS

Tucks are small, stitched folds which may vary greatly in width. They may be worked on either the right or wrong side of the garment and perform the following functions:

1 They dispose of fullness and introduce shaping, e.g. on shoulders of blouse.

2 They can be used to take up extra width and length which may later require letting out, e.g. on children's garments.

3 They are useful for decoration, e.g. pin-tucks on a bodice front.

Tucks other than pin-tucks, like pleats, take up three times their finished width of material.

They are best worked on a straight thread of material, but as they are usually quite narrow they may be worked quite successfully in most directions.

Pin-tucks

These are no more than the width of a pin wide and may be worked without tacking first. If required, a thread of the material may be drawn out as a guide for the fold of the tuck.

Working

1 Fold material along required line of pin-tuck and stitch very close to the fold.

2 Bring both machine-threads to the same side, thread into a large-eyed needle and run it back through the tuck far enough to secure a strong finish.

If shaped pin-tucks are required they should be marked out with tacking stitches before being sewn.

Pin-tucks may be worked by hand if desired, very fine running stitches being worked. Backstitching is not suitable as both sides of the stitching are visible.

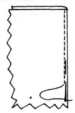

Direction of stitch and needle

Wider Tucks

Tucks may be spaced or lie close to each other.

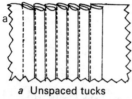

a Unspaced tucks

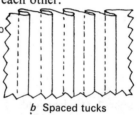

b Spaced tucks

a Unspaced tucks

In this method the fold of the first tuck sets the line for the stitching of the second tuck, and so on.

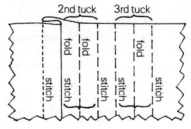

b Spaced tucks

Make a guide to show the depth of the tuck required and the width of the space between.

Use the guide to mark the tucks as shown.

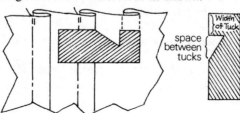

space between tucks

Width of Tuck

All tucks may be gauged if preferred by using the tuck guide provided by most sewing-machine manufacturers. This is screwed to the base of the machine at the required distance from the foot. Clear directions for the use of this and other attachments are given in the handbook provided by the maker.

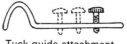

Tuck guide attachment

Finishing tucks

1 After tucks have been stitched they should be turned in the direction desired, according to the finished effect required.

2 Fastening off of the machine-ends must be worked on the inside or underside of the tuck.

PLEATS

A pleat is a fold of material designed to give extra width in garments. It consists of three layers of material, so for each pleat three times the required finish width is needed (e.g. for a 5 cm pleat, 15 cm of material is required), plus the distance required between pleats, if any.

Pleats may be left to hang free from a supporting band or they may be stitched for part of their length to give a closer fit.

Pleats hang most satisfactorily if they are formed on the selvedge threads of the material.

Material may now be bought permanently pleated and may also be commercially pleated to order by specialized firms.

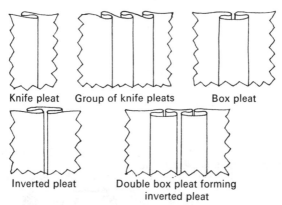

Knife pleat   Group of knife pleats   Box pleat

Inverted pleat   Double box pleat forming inverted pleat

Marking

On paper patterns, the lines of pleats are always shown for their entire length and these lines should be carefully marked on the material. Two different coloured threads should be used for this purpose, one to indicate the fold of the pleat and one to show the line to which the fold is to be placed.

Marking and tacking of pleats is most satisfactorily worked with the material laid out flat on a table. An ironing board is a good substitute for a table.

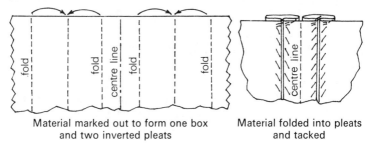

Material marked out to form one box
and two inverted pleats

Material folded into pleats
and tacked

If pleats are to be stitched part-way they may be edge-stitched on the right side with or without a seam.

Top-stitched Pleats
Prepare as for above effect and edge-stitch both edges and across as shown.

Arrowheads may be worked if required. These give a smart finish and help to prevent the pleat from breaking away.

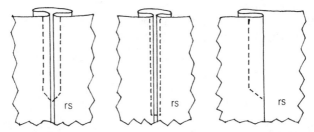

Note: The folded edges of pleats may be edge-stitched on right and/or wrong side. This helps to keep the pleat in position.
Working an arrowhead
Mark out shape with small tacking stitches. Using buttonhole twist, work arrowhead as indicated in the diagram.

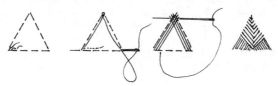

Inside-stitched Pleats

    1 Place the right sides of the material together, fold line to fold line, and tack the complete length of the pleat (this should already have been tailor-tacked).

    2 Stitch to required length of fitted portion of pleat. Fasten off securely, either by using the reverse feed on the machine or by pulling through and darning in the ends. The latter method strengthens the end of the stitching at a place where otherwise it can very easily be broken away.

    3 Lay out the stitched material right side downwards on a table with the fold line of the pleat lying directly over the stitched seam. Pin and tack into position. Remove the pins.

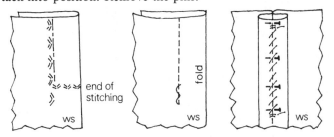

    4 Place a damp cloth over the pleat on the wrong side and press firmly. Do not iron backwards and forwards. Press on the fabric as lightly as possible. Lift the iron and repeat until the entire pleat has been pressed. To prevent the pleat impression from the wrong side marking the right side of the material slip a piece of thick paper between the pleat and the garment.

    Remove the tacking threads and press firmly once more to remove any stitch marks.

    5 Work arrowhead or edge-stitching as required.

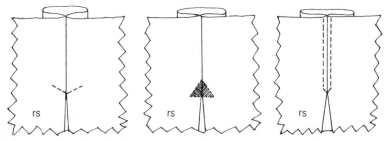

Note: Although an inverted pleat is shown in these diagrams similar methods may be used for knife and box pleats.

    Some materials, such as tweeds, may give too bulky an effect for a good fit. If this is the case the extra inner layer of material may be cut away above the free pleat, on one thickness. In this case the edges must be neatened and the pleat supported to prevent it from dropping below the hem line as its weight stretches the threads.

Method of cutting away and neatening extra material

A

1 Cut down the inside folds of the pleat to 2·5 cm above the end of stitching.

2 Cut away shaded portion (i.e. all but 2·5 cm each side of stitched line and 2·5 cm above end of stitching). Neaten raw edges.

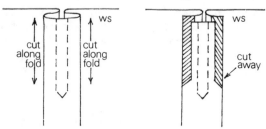

B

1 For deep pleats in bulky material which are not supported by top stitching, work a line of stitching down the sewing line and out to the inner fold at right angles.

2 Cut down the fold to within 2·5 cm of the horizontal stitching and trim away inner layer (shaded area) to within 2·5 cm of seam.

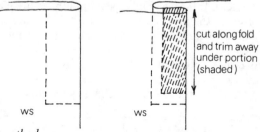

Alternative method

1 Cut away top portion of pleat only (shaded portion) and stitch raw edges.

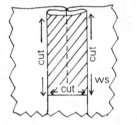
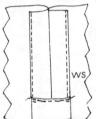

2 Cut a rectangle of lining 2·5 cm wider and 1·3 cm longer than piece cut away. Fold 1·3 cm turnings to the wrong side as shown. Tack.

3 Place wrong side of lining to inside of pleat, tack into position. Fasten sides of lining to cut edge of pleat turning and hem lower edge to inner thickness of pleat.

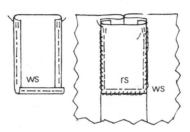

Method for hem of pleat where there is a seam
In a gored and pleated skirt the seam often forms the inner fold of the pleat. It then makes the hem too bulky to be turned up in the usual way and the following method should be used.

1 Top and bottom section of seamed pleat.

If possible leave seam merely tacked until after the hem has been fixed. Then stitch and neaten the seam for its entire length.

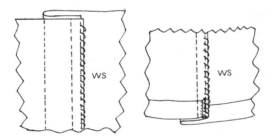

2 If seam has already been stitched, undo it for depth of hem and then re-stitch the seam as in 1.

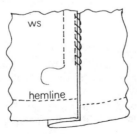

EASING

This is a method of manipulating curved seams and fullness in sleeve heads. Balance marks must be accurately matched and care should be taken not to overhandle and therefore stretch the fabric. Press carefully over a tailor's ham or soft pad.

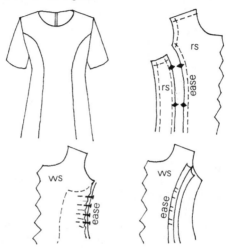

FURTHER STUDY

THINGS TO DO

1 Work specimens of gathering, tucking (three types), pleating and smocking (see p. 168).

2 Prepare folders of each process, including uses of each.

3 Collect illustrations of the use of each method.

QUESTIONS TO ANSWER

1 Complete the following statements by filling in the blanks with words taken from the right-hand column.

a When gathers are required .... rows of stitching should be worked and pulled up together.	wrong
	tuck
b If embroidery stitches are worked over rows of gathers the result is known as	dart
c When a piece of fabric is to be pleated .... the finished width is to be allowed for each pleat.	easing
d Fullness allowed for a curve can be reduced and shaped at the same time by means of a .... tapered at one or at both ends.	smocking
	two

e If it is not tapered the fold of fabric becomes a ....

f A pleat which is a single fold stitched for part of its length *or* left free for its full length is called a .... pleat.

g A box pleat has both creased edges visible on the .... side of the garment.

h An inverted pleat resembles a box pleat on the .... side.

i The fullness at the top of a sleeve or at an elbow can be reduced by ....

j For good results in gathering .... the width of the finished measurement should be allowed.

twice

three times

knife

right

2*a* Name *five* ways in which fullness may be controlled when making garments.

b Describe how two methods are worked, one method by machine and one by hand. Give diagrams.   (A.E.B.)

3 Describe, with illustrations, the difference between tucks and pleats, naming *two* examples of each.   (A.E.B.)

4 Sketch two different types of pleats and state where each can be suitably used. Describe the planning and working of one of them.

(A.E.B.)

5 Show exactly how you would shorten the hem of a pleated woollen skirt. Illustrate your answer with labelled diagrams.

3

GARMENT-MAKING

CHOICE OF MATERIAL

Today there is a very great number of different materials available and manufacturers are still working to produce new and improved fabrics. Many processes which add to the value of the materials (finishes resulting in crease-resistance, stain repulsion, washability of wool, etc.) are now in common use. More detailed descriptions of these will be found in Chapter 8.

Choosing the material for a garment you are going to make your-self can be quite exciting, and this choice should be given careful consideration. Whether the material is chosen to suit the pattern or the style first and material later is largely a matter of circumstances. For instance, a present of a dress-length may be received and a pattern will have to be found which requires just that amount of material as well as being suitable in other ways for the fabric in hand; or there may be a need for a new garment, in which case it is usual to choose a style first and then to buy the required amount of suitable material. In either case, some knowledge of the characteristics of the more common fabrics is of great assistance if really satisfactory results are to be obtained.

For beginners, materials should be used which, while being pleasing to the eye, are easy to handle. It is most discouraging to a keen but inexperienced needlewoman to have to wrestle with difficult fabrics —those which fray easily, lack body, are limp, easily creased and, in these days of mass-produced clothes, not worth spending time to make up. Knowledge of how to deal with and manipulate different fabrics can only be obtained from practical experience but this should be acquired gradually and skill in managing simple fabrics achieved first.

It is important to learn the 'feel' of the various materials likely to be used and one of the most useful ways of doing this is to test materials on show in drapery stores by checking their weight in the hand and squeezing them gently to assess their crease-resistance. Under the Trade Descriptions Act, labels of fabrics on display should give accurate information, and verbal descriptions given by shop assistants should be correct. Inaccurate labelling is an offence which can be reported to the local Weights and Measures Department. Prices should also be noted and reasons for variations in cost appreciated. For instance, two cotton fabrics which appear very similar in weave, colour, design and weight may show a considerable difference in price. On investigation it may be found that one has been treated in such a way that it is labelled 'drip-dry' or 'crease-resistant' while the other has had no special finish, or they may be of different widths.

A word of warning—most assistants in fabric departments are usually very willing to give information such as is described above, *but* they are not pleased to have goods handled by gloved or grimy fingers!

Prices of fabrics bought by the metre vary a great deal so that there is a good range of attractive materials to suit most purses. It is a good principle always to buy the best material that can be afforded and to remember that a good cotton is preferable to a more glamorous but shoddy rayon of the same price.

There are certain processes involved in the manufacture of some fabrics which add to the cost of an otherwise reasonably priced cloth:

Woven patterns as opposed to printed ones
In the former the design is apparent on both sides of the cloth and cannot wash or wear off; in the latter the design is only stamped on the right side and may be impaired with wear.

Screen printing
In this method each colour of the design is printed separately through stencils.

Metallic threads incorporated into the material
These are actually plastic-covered aluminium filaments which retain their lustre and colour even in washing and are popular for evening and cocktail dress fabrics.

Exclusive designs
There is a growing custom of engaging well-known artists to design fabrics and, in these cases, when copyright designs are produced, the price of the finished material is naturally increased.

Special finishes
These include embossing, tebelizing, sanforizing, and treating surfaces in order that they may drip-dry or become crease, stain and/or moisture repellent. (See p. 220.)

CHARACTERISTICS OF FABRICS

COTTON

Cotton materials nowadays range from the finest organdies to the heaviest denims. Some of the most widely used materials and finishes are as follows:

Plain, Even Weave
(For uses of these fabrics see table on pp. 90–4. For diagram of even-weave see p. 50.)

Calico: a very strong, easily-handled material, plain white or unbleached.

Organdie: this is a lightweight, semi-transparent material with a crisp finish. It loses its stiffness in laundering but regains it if ironed while very damp.

Poplin: in weaving this material the weft threads used are slightly thicker than the closely-packed warp, giving a very finely corded effect. It launders very easily and wears well.

Voile: this is rather like a more finely-textured lawn, very soft but quite firm. It is a material which is very popular nowadays, in plain and printed designs and in cotton synthetic blends. These keep their shape and crispness well. It is evenly woven but may have chenille bobbles or checks incorporated, when it is known as 'dotted swiss'.

Gingham: this is always a very popular cotton material, as it is strong, attractive and easily laundered. It is woven with coloured threads to produce stripes, checks and plaids. The main check may be outlined in heavier or looped threads, and is then known as 'seerloop gingham'.

Winceyette: the surface of the material is fluffy and soft on both right and wrong sides. It is a very popular material for nightwear particularly for children, but has the disadvantage of being highly inflammable. Care must be taken to buy only fabric which has a flame-resistant finish (e.g. Proban or Lo-Flam).

A more modern version of this material has the napped surface on the wrong side only, giving additional cosiness next to the skin but avoiding the tendency to 'pill' or form small balls of fluff on the right side.

Twilled Weave

This is a weave in which the weft threads are passed over two or more warp threads and under one in each row of weaving, giving a diagonally-marked appearance to the completed fabric. This makes a very strong material such as *denim*, or some *cotton gaberdines*.

Corded Weave

Piqué: is an example. At regular intervals the weft threads form filling floats at the back of the warp threads. Also, between each section, there is a wider space than usual between the warp threads so that a corded effect is achieved. The cords may be introduced in one direction only or in both directions. When they cross each other, forming squares, the material is known as *waffle piqué*. The fabric is very hard-wearing and easily laundered. It should be ironed on the wrong side.

Cheaper forms of this material with the same appearance are produced with an embossed finish.

Corduroy: this fabric is woven with extra floating weft yarns which form lengthwise ribs. These are later cut to form pile cords. This fabric must be drip-dried and should not be twisted or wrung, which will damage the pile. Press face downwards onto the pile of a piece of spare material.

Other Weaves
Crepon: a crinkled-effect fabric with fine, regular, bark-like ribs running with the warp. Sometimes known as 'tree-bark', it is a drip-dry material which must not be ironed.

WOOL

Like cotton fabrics, woollen materials vary from very fine lacy textures to heavy, blanket-like ones, including a great many weights and finishes between the two. (See pp. 210–13.) Wool cloth is divided into two types: the woollens made from short, loosely-spun fibres, giving surface interest, and the worsteds made from longer better-quality fibres, giving a close, smooth, firm surface.

Plain, Even Weave
Flannel: a slightly napped, soft fabric which is very hard-wearing and pleats beautifully. This may be a 'woollen' material when the napped surface hides the weave, or a 'worsted flannel' when the weave is still visible.
Wool/angora blends: the addition of a small percentage of angora fibres makes a soft fabric with attractive, irregular surface hairs.

Twilled Weave
Gaberdine: a very firmly woven worsted fabric with an obvious diagonal corded effect. It is extremely hard-wearing and keeps its shape well; the surface is quite smooth.
Houndstooth check: this is made with even numbers of threads in two colours. The twilled weave gives a jagged-tooth effect. It may also be called 'puppy-tooth' (very small checks) or 'dog-tooth' (medium-sized checks).

Other Weaves
Tweed: a light, medium or heavy material, woven in one or more colours, ranging from smooth, soft West of England cloth to coarse-textured Harris. The weave may be plain, twilled or herringboned. It is a hard-wearing material and one which never goes out of fashion.
Barathea: a very hard-wearing, smooth-surfaced material with a slightly granular appearance due to the threads of one direction being somewhat thicker than those of the other.
Crêpe: a light, springy material with a matt, crinkled surface due to the use of highly twisted crêpe weft yarns (worsted).
Bouclé: a light, medium or heavy-weight material with a knobbly surface due to the use of looped twisted yarns. It is not suitable for pleating.

SILK

Most silk materials are too expensive for amateurs to use, although they are, of course, attractive and easy to handle. There are versions in pure silk of most rayon materials (velvet, taffeta, crêpe, satin, etc.). Two characteristic silk fabrics are tussore and Jap silk, which are attractive and simple to work on. (See p. 215.)

LINEN

Dress linens are somewhat expensive, but they are hard-wearing and attractive. The weave is usually quite plain but can be woven with a slubbed yarn to give a textured effect and the fabric has its own natural lustre and slight stiffness. (See pp. 92 and 222.)

MAN-MADE FABRICS

All man-made fibres have their own lustre and are therefore slippery to handle, but during manufacture a 'de-lustring' process is used to produce matt-finished fabric. The range of man-made fabrics is now enormous. (See pp. 228–31.)

Plain, Even Weave

Chiffon (rayon, nylon): a very thin, soft, delicate material which drapes and gathers particularly well.

Taffeta (rayon, nylon): has a sheen on both right and wrong sides and the weave has a very finely ribbed appearance. It often has a 'shot' effect and must then be cut with all pieces in the same direction. It can also be water-marked under pressure and is then known as 'moiré taffeta'.

Lining: usually a plain weave fabric, although there are twill, crêpe and satin types, in rayon, tricel, dicel or nylon. It is used to line or mount garments.

Fancy Weaves

Crêpe (tricel, terylene): this is a fine crinkled, rather springy material with a similar appearance on both sides.

Surah/foulard: a lightweight twill weave fabric, usually printed. It was originally made from silk but is now mainly made from tricel or modified rayons.

Satin: a double-sided material with a smooth, shiny right side and a dull back. It may be obtained in many weights from a very thin, rather poor quality to a thick 'duchess' satin.

NYLON

Materials made from nylon filaments may now be obtained in many different weights and weaves. Although they are fairly expensive, their advantages usually outweigh the disadvantage of the initial cost. Nylon is not an easy material to handle and should not be used until the worker is quite experienced. (See p. 230.)

KNITTED FABRICS

'Jersey' is a term very widely used to describe knitted materials, the weave being that of the old-fashioned 'lock-knit' fabrics. This material may be knitted from cotton, rayon, silk, wool or nylon, but again it is not an easy material to work on and should be avoided by all but very skilled needlewomen. (See pp. 92 and 213–4.) They may be produced as warp or weft knits.

In warp knits the yarn is carried up through the fabric in the warp direction. This gives stability and does not ladder. Weft knits are produced in a similar manner to hand knitting and provide a soft, easily draped fabric. These may be produced in cotton, Tricel, Dicel, Courtelle, Acrilan, and bulked fibres such as Crimplene and Banlon, as plain, printed or Jaquard fabrics.

PILE AND BRUSHED FABRICS

Velvet (rayon, rayon/cotton, nylon): the weft threads are interlaced through a double warp beam and are then cut to form two rolls of pile. Rayon pile velvets are normally worked on a cotton back.

This material must be cut with all the pieces in the same direction. To determine the correct direction of cutting, hold the length of material against the body and look down it. If the surface shows only the sheen of the fabric it is not such a strong colour but the garment will wear well. If the colour is clearly defined, giving a rich effect, the fabric is not so hard-wearing and this method of cutting is most suitable for evening wear. An alternative test for correct direction is to stroke the pile and feel whether the hand is smoothing down or pushing against it.

Fleece fabrics: pile fabrics made from Courtelle, Acrilan, Orlon, nylon or Teklan to imitate fleece or furs, e.g. simulated pony skin, coney or leopard.

Brushed fabrics: after the fabric has been manufactured (either woven or knitted) a non-directional surface nap is raised by brushing on either the right or wrong side, or, for additional warmth, on both sides, e.g.

brushed rayon: made to imitate plain weave wool fabrics and provide a cheaper alternative.

brushed nylon: a knitted fabric brushed on the right side, it provides a 'lo-flam' material for nightwear.

napped cotton: see winceyette.

Teklan: can be made in a form that is similar in appearance to brushed nylon, but is a modified acrylic fibre. It has a reduced fire risk for nightwear as, unlike nylon, it does not drip when burnt.

D

Summary of Characteristics and Use of Familiar Fabrics

Code Letters B = Suitable for beginners; M = Suitable for semi-skilled workers;
D = Difficult to handle, suitable for skilled workers only.

Fabric	Width	Fibre	Uses	Characteristics	Laundering Points	Code Letter
Afgalaine	140 cm	Wool, rayon	Dresses, jumper suits	Suitable for almost any style of garment—tailored, casual, etc. Pleats, gathers and tucks well Frays if very loosely woven Creases badly	Not suitable for washing as inclined to shrink Shines if not pressed carefully	M
Bouclé	140 cm 150 cm	Wool	Dresses, suits, coats	Hangs well and will drape if lightweight Does not crease Will not pleat If very pronounced bouclé weave, stitching is sometimes difficult to keep straight (as in velvet, two surfaces 'walk' against each other)	Suitable for dry-cleaning only	M to D
Brushed nylon	90 cm 115 cm 150 cm	Nylon	Nightwear	Warm to handle Does not fray Flame-resistant	Warm wash, drip-dry	M to D
Brushed rayon	90 cm	Viscose rayon	Dresses, blouses, children's garments	Soft, warm to handle Creases Not hard-wearing	Warm wash, drip-dry, press lightly	B
Calico	90 cm 100 cm 180 cm	Cotton	Interfacing, household goods	Hard-wearing Shrinks Creases badly Will remain in place without slipping Does not fray 'Dressing' makes surface a little stiff Fine sewing cannot be worked	Easily washed in hot water, starch if necessary White calico can be boiled May be pulled into shape while wet Iron on either side while still damp, using hot iron	B

Fabric	Width	Fibre	Uses	Characteristics	Care	Code
Chiffon	90 cm 115 cm	Rayon, nylon, silk	Blouses, nightdresses, evening wear, trimmings	Hangs, drapes and gathers well Suitable for fine sewing Requires skilled handling as very delicate Frays	Wash in warm soapy water Press with warm iron	D
Corduroy	70 cm 90 cm	Cotton	Dresses, housecoats, suits, coats, jeans, children's clothes	Hard-wearing Firm to handle Has a nap	Wash or dry-clean Drip-dry Do not wring	M
Cotton satin	90 cm	Cotton, vincel, cotton/vincel	Dresses, skirts, shirts, blouses	Firm to handle Keeps shape well Does not fray Hangs well Will gather and tuck Often crease-resisting Presses well	Washes easily in hand-hot water Iron while slightly damp on right side Repels dirt owing to shiny surface	B
Crêpe	90 cm 115 cm	Wool, rayon, tricel, silk	Blouses, lingerie, dresses	Gathers, drapes, tucks and hangs well May be successfully embroidered Somewhat springy Must be pressed on wrong side to avoid glazing	Most true crêpes should be dry-cleaned If washed, use warm, soapy water Press dry or very slightly evenly damp on wrong side with warm iron Do not 'damp down'	M to D
Crepon	90 cm 115 cm	Cotton	Blouses, dresses, slips	Comfortable to wear Non-iron easy care	Must not be ironed	M
Denim	90 cm 120 cm	Cotton, rayon	Shorts, jeans, shirts, overalls, dresses, children's wear (according to weight of fabric)	Very firm, hard-wearing material Usually reversible Does not fray Cannot be gathered satisfactorily	Launder according to fibre content	B to M
Flannel	70 cm 140 cm	Wool, wool/rayon, wool/cotton	Skirts, suits, dresses, shorts	Pleats well Hangs well Firm to handle Suitable for tailored styles Does not fray	Wash in warm, soapy water Press on wrong side	M
Foulard *See Surah*						

Fabric	Width	Fibre	Uses	Characteristics	Laundering Points	Code Letter
Gaberdine	90 cm 140 cm 150 cm	Wool, cotton	Suits, skirts, jackets, coats, dresses, raincoats	Suitable for all tailored styles Pleats well Firm to handle	Cotton gaberdine may be washed Otherwise dry-clean Keep well brushed	M
Georgette	90 cm 115 cm	Rayon, nylon, silk	Blouses, lingerie, dresses, trimming	Suitable for fine sewing Drapes and gathers well Does not fray easily Crêpe-like texture causes seams and edges to stretch and flute	*See Chiffon*	D
Gingham	90 cm	Cotton, cotton/terylene, rayon	Children's garments, housecoats, overalls, beachwear, dresses	Woven check Easy to handle Easy to press Does not pleat Gathers well Very suitable for smocking	Wash in hot, soapy water May be starched if extra stiffness is required Presses well on either side while damp	B
Houndstooth check	140 cm	Wool, wool/rayon, wool/terylene	Dresses, coats, suits	Light, medium or heavyweight Other characteristics vary with fibre content	Dry-clean	M
Jersey fabrics	90 cm 140 cm 150 cm	Cotton, tricel, Crimplene, Courtelle, Acrilan, Orlon, nylon, wool	Dresses, blouses, skirts, suits	Hangs and drapes well Stretches on cut edges and must be handled carefully to avoid pulling out of shape	Warm wash man-made fibres Dry-clean wool Drip-dry Crimplene Do not drip-dry Orlon (liable to stretch) Press Courtelle when dry only	M to D
Lawn	90 cm	Cotton, terylene, tricel	Lingerie, blouses, dresses	Slightly polished Easily worked Does not fray Presses easily Suitable for gathering	Easily washed in hot water May be pulled into shape while wet Starch if necessary Iron on either side while still damp, using hot iron	B
Linen	90 cm 115 cm	Linen, linen/terylene blend to reduce creasing	Dresses, suits, skirts	Hangs and pleats well Firm to sew, keeps shape well Presses easily Suitable for tailored garments Frays, sometimes badly Creases badly unless specially treated	Will wash and press well Should be ironed on wrong side	M

Fabric	Width	Fibre	Uses	Properties	Care	
Moiré taffeta	90 cm 115 cm	Rayon	Evening dresses	*See Taffeta* Watermark pattern which must be matched at seams	Dry-clean	D
Organdie	90 cm 100 cm	Cotton	Blouses, children's dresses, trimming, interfacing	Suitable for fine sewing, tucking, rolled hems, hand embroidery Frays slightly Transparent and so requires special processes, i.e. French seams, double hems	May be washed and ironed easily Must be ironed while damp to restore crispness May be starched if necessary Shrinks	B to M
Piqué	90 cm	Cotton, man-made fibres	Blouses, shirts, shorts, jackets, dresses, summer coats	Firm to handle Does not fray Wears well Keeps shape well Does not gather	Launders well Crispness may be restored with thin starch Iron while damp, on wrong side	B
Poplin	90 cm	Cotton, rayon	Blouses, children's wear, shirts, dresses, raincoats	Firm to handle Does not fray Suitable for gathering	Wash in hot water May be pulled into shape while wet Drip-dry Press lightly	B
Satin	90 cm 115 cm	Rayon, nylon, silk	Evening wear, blouses, lingerie, nightwear	Hangs well May be gathered, tucked, embroidered Drapes well Frays easily Slips unless firmly tacked	Lingerie satins may be washed in warm, soapy water Iron on right side while still damp Avoid 'damping down' as this causes 'spotting'	D
Seersucker	90 cm	Cotton, nylon	Blouses, dresses, children's wear, lingerie	Easily to handle Little pressing required except for seams Gathers and hangs well Cannot be pleated or tucked	Simple to launder Drip-dry	B
Surah/Foulard	90 cm 115 cm	Tricel, silk	Dresses, blouses, scarves	Lightweight Drapes well	Hand-wash Drip-dry Press when evenly damp	M
Taffeta	90 cm	Rayon, nylon	Petticoats, dresses, blouses	Hangs well when gathered or flared Retains crispness Sometimes frays badly	Rayon cannot be washed satisfactorily, should be dry-cleaned Press on wrong side to avoid glaze on right side	D

Fabric	Width	Fibre	Uses	Characteristics	Laundering Points	Code Letter
Tweed	70 cm 140 cm 150 cm	Wool, wool/rayon	Suits, skirts, coats, dresses, jackets	Does not crease easily Holds pleats Frays if very loosely woven	Suitable for dry-cleaning only Keep well brushed	M to D
Velvet	70 cm 90 cm	Rayon, cotton, nylon	Dresses, jackets, housecoats	Drapes and hangs well Can be cut in one direction only One surface 'walks' against another so must be firmly fixed Best sewn by hand Press on 'velvet board' 'Pin' with needles	Must be dry cleaned Press on 'velvet board' or with iron standing on end and wrong side of material passed across it	D
Voile	90 cm 115 cm	Cotton, nylon, other man-made fibres	Blouses, children's wear, dresses	Transparent—see Organdie Drapes easily Frays Suitable for fine sewing, tucking, frilling	Washes and irons easily Iron while damp	D
Winceyette	90 cm	Cotton	Nightwear	Does not fray Presses easily Firm to handle Somewhat bulky Clumsy for working Highly inflammable unless specially treated	Inclined to shrink Wash in warm, soapy water Iron dry or slightly damp	M
Wool/Angora blends	140 cm 175 cm	Wool with small percentage of angora	Dresses, light suits	May be woven or knitted (jersey) Warm, lightweight Crease-resistant Holds pleats	Dry-clean	M
Worsted	140 cm 150 cm	Wool	Suits, skirts, coats, jackets, dresses	Suitable for all tailored styles Pleats well Firm to handle	Suitable for dry-cleaning only Keep well brushed	M

BLENDS AND MIXTURES

Many present-day materials are combinations of two or more quite different textile fibres (e.g. Terylene/worsted, Terylene/cotton, rayon or wool). Sometimes the fibres are combined before the yarn is spun (a blend or blended fabric) and sometimes the warp threads are of one type and the weft of another (a mixture).

These blends and mixtures combine the advantages of both threads while usually minimizing their disadvantages, e.g. a Terylene and cotton blend has the easy-care, drip-dry, minimum-iron and crease-resistant properties of Terylene and the absorbency and comfort of cotton. If the fabric has 55% or more synthetic fibre it takes on thermoplastic properties, i.e. it can be permanently pleated.

As far as the laundering of these blends and mixtures is concerned, if there is a any wool content, treat as for wool; other blends should be treated as for their man-made content, e.g. if a Terylene/cotton is washed or pressed as a cotton the Terylene may gain irremovable heat-set creases if wrung or spun-dried when warm, and may discolour or disintegrate if pressed at temperatures suitable for cotton.

ADDITIONAL MATERIALS

Interfacings
Used for interfacing collars, cuffs, belts and facings and interlining skirts, jackets and dresses to give a crisp, tailored line.
Tailor's canvas: suitable for jackets and coats. Will clean safely.
Organdie: a suitable interfacing for all lightweight materials, e.g. printed and plain lawns, poplin and light wools.
Taffeta: nylon or rayon taffeta can be used as an interlining to help retain shape and give body.
Bonded fibre fabrics (*Vilene, Oswalene, Lantor, Solena*): these are suitable for all interfacing and interlining purposes because they are washable, cannot fray, and are available in many weights in black, white and grey. They can be cut in any direction, having no woven threads.

Belt Backing
Now available in black and white washable material in 2–5 cm widths. Belts can be made very successfully at home, and professional-looking results easily achieved with the buckle-making outfits also available.

Petersham
A firm strip interfacing suitable for skirt-bands. Available in several widths and colours, straight and curved. A 100% Terylene version is available which will wash successfully.

Shoulder Pads
These may be purchased covered or non-covered, and in sizes and shapes

suitable for coats, jackets, dresses. They are only used when fashion demands a very square shoulder line. Some are manufactured from layers of canvas and fibre. These will dry-clean with the garment, and are usually used for coats and jackets. Lighter-weight shaped pads are available manufactured from foam rubber or plastic. These will wash but should be removed before dry-cleaning.

Threads

Cotton (fine, medium, coarse), Sylko, pure silk, Trylko, Drima: used according to the material.

Buttonhole twist: for working buttonholes on coats and jackets, arrowheads and decorative stitching. It is thicker and firmer than silk.

Tacking cotton: a soft, easily broken thread which does not mark the material.

HINTS FOR CHOOSING MATERIALS

The material should be:

    1 *Within the worker's ability to handle.* See charts on pp. 90–4.

    2 *Suitable for the garment required.* Most pattern envelopes give suggestions for suitable fabrics and the worker should be guided by these. As has already been seen, some materials pleat, gather and hang better than others and care must be taken not to buy crisp materials for soft, draped effects; napped materials for a style including tucks; springy ones for fully gathered styles; or easily fraying fabrics for a design including many buttonholes.

    3 *Suitable for the wearer.* Here it is important to know the good and bad points of one's figure and to use materials which disguise the poor features and enhance the good ones. Personal colouring must also be taken into consideration:

        a for plump, full figures avoid shiny materials

        b for tall, thin figures avoid vertical stripes

        c for short, bulky figures avoid large designs.

    4 *Of the right colour.* This should blend in with the other garments in the wearer's wardrobe: a coat must not clash (even if it is of a different colour, it may still go well with other garments) with the main colours worn; a suit should be of a colour suitable for wearing under a top-coat or over blouses and jumpers already purchased; a skirt should be of a colour which will set off the wearer's blouses, jackets, etc. A drastic change of colour scheme usually involves replacing more accessories than can comfortably be afforded at one time.

    Personal choice here is a great factor but do not be afraid to experiment with colour and design: many fabrics, particularly blue, grey and mauve ones, change their appearance slightly under artificial light. Evening fabrics, particularly, should be chosen in the light in which they will most often be worn, to avoid later disappointment.

5 *Easily washed or cleaned*, according to the amount of wear they are likely to have. If the garment is to be washed, it is important to choose interfacing, lining and trimmings which are washable; if it is to be dry-cleaned particular attention should be paid to the choice of buttons, buckles and belts.

6 *Of a suitable weave for the garment:* on the whole it is a good rule to choose closely-woven fabrics (particularly wools) for closely fitted garments; loosely-woven materials may have to be mounted to keep their shape when used for fitted styles.

7 *Of a reasonable price* for the importance of the garment and the amount of time and work involved in the making: the amount of money paid for the material should be in proportion to the amount of wear it is expected to give: a top-coat which will give several years' service should be made from better quality material than a summer dress which will be worn for a very short time and will probably be discarded before it is completely worn out.

DESIGNS ON MATERIAL

Striking, large designs, whether plaids, stripes or floral patterns, can look very effective—used with care. If badly arranged, however, the amateurish effect obtained completely ruins even the best sewn garment.

When cutting out the material, the pieces of pattern must be so arranged that stripes match at all seams. Careful thought must be given to striped materials before cutting.

Large groups of flowers or large single motifs should be evenly arranged on each side of the garment, e.g. in the middle of each sleeve, one on each shoulder.

The arrangement of the patterns on some materials is such that it can be used in either direction and these are known as 'all-over' designs. Some, however, are obviously meant to be used in one way only and in this case care must be taken when cutting out to see that each part of the pattern is cut with the design running in the same direction. (See p. 112.)

This method of cutting means that the pattern cannot be cut as economically as on all-over designs and allowance must be made for this when buying the length of material. (Measures required for one-way or napped materials are now often given on pattern envelopes, as well as the normal amounts required.)

Large-motif designs should be avoided by short people, not only by plump ones but also by slightly built ones. They have a somewhat swamping effect on both types of short figures, drawing attention to generous curves and overwhelming small bones.

A well defined, formal design should be used on styles with as few seams as possible, otherwise the beauty of the motif is lost by being cut up in too many places.

ESTIMATING AMOUNTS

All commercial patterns show clearly on their covers exactly how much material is required for any specified garment. In some circumstances, however (perhaps when budgeting for replacements in one's wardrobe), it is convenient to know how much material is required for making a certain garment or what garments can be made from a certain length of material.

Most fabrics are woven in 90 cm, 115 cm and 140 cm widths; cottons, rayons, nylons and other fine fabrics being 90 cm or 115 cm wide, while woven woollens and other heavier materials are 140 cm wide.

Knitted fabrics are usually 150 cm wide and handwoven ones 70 cm wide.

PERSONAL MEASUREMENTS

1 It is advisable to have one's measurements taken by a friend, if possible, so that there is no danger of the tape sagging at any point.

2 Use a firm, fibre-glass tape measure for accurate measurements.

3 Take measurements over well-fitting foundation garments.

4 Make a note of the measurements taken, widths first, then lengths.

5 Measurements should be checked regularly.

Method

1 Bust: place the tape round the fullest part of the figure, well up across the back, taking a close measurement.

2 Waist: place the tape comfortably round the natural waist.

3 Hips: place the tape closely round the fullest part of the seat. The depth of this measurement below the waist varies according to figure type and height.

4 Back width: at a point halfway down the armhole, measure across the back.

5 Shoulder to waist: place the tape from the shoulder close to the neck, over the bust, to the natural waist.

6 Back neck to waist: measure from nape bone at back of neck to centre-back natural waist.

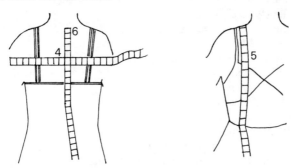

7 Skirt length: place tape at natural waist above hip-bone and measure over hip to normal skirt-length.

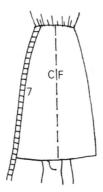

8 Long sleeve: measure from point of shoulder to wrist with the elbow bent. With the elbow bent, measure round the thickest part of the upper arm. Measure round the wrist.

9 Short sleeve: measure from arm-pit to required length down inside of arm, with arm raised. Measure round thickest part of upper arm.

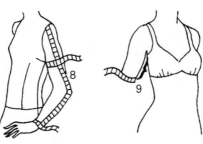

AMOUNTS REQUIRED

The amount of material required depends on:.

    a the style of garment

    b the size of the wearer

    c the width of the material.

Certain things will, however, add to the amount necessary:

    a wide stripes or checks which must be matched (p. 112)

    b 'one-way' materials (p. 112)

    c large masses of pattern

    d extra length required for tall figures.

When estimating amounts remember that:

    a selvedge or warp threads run downwards on most sections of garments, therefore length is most important when gauging approximate amounts

    b up to 80 cm bust size, bodices can be cut completely from one width of 90 cm material (10 cm allowed for ease in wearing and for turnings).

    c 5–7·5 cm must be added to the length for seams and hems.

Estimating Amount for Short-sleeved Blouse, Tunic or Jacket
(87–92 cm bust and 90 cm material)

Bodice sections

Longer portion of the bodice (the front) requires the measurement from shoulder to waist+15 cm tuck-in or minimum overlap, seam and hem allowance:

    approximately 45 cm+15 cm = 60 cm.

The front and back pattern pieces may be overlapped for their narrowest parts (from shoulder to bottom of armhole), approximately 22·5 cm.

    ∴ length required for complete bodice is $(2 \times 60 \text{ cm}) - 22 \cdot 5 \text{ cm} =$
    97·5 cm.

(Amount required for sleeveless blouse = 97·5 cm+20 cm for facings and collar = 117·5 cm. Amount of material purchased is 1·2 m.)

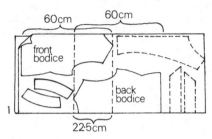

Sleeves

Width of sleeve will be less than half the width of the fabric and therefore sleeves can be cut from doubled fabric, i.e. 45 cm.

∴ only one length of sleeve is required, approximately 22·5 cm from head to hem.

Sleeve pattern may overlap facing pattern approximately 7·5 cm.

∴ amount required = 22·5 cm−7·5 cm = 15 cm.

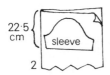

Facings

These will be the same length as the front bodice and will fit beside the lower portion of the back bodice.

∴ approximately 20 cm will be required (as for sleeveless blouse).

Collar and Cuffs

These will be cut from fabric left beside other pattern pieces and no extra fabric need be allowed.

∴ complete amount required = 97·5 cm+15 cm+20 cm = 132·5 cm.

Amount of fabric to be purchased is 1·4 m.

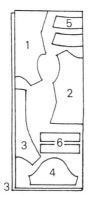

1 Front bodice
2 Back bodice
3 Facing
4 Sleeve
5 Collar (double)
6 Cuffs

Estimating Amount for Long-sleeved Blouse, Tunic or Jacket

The difference in the length of fabric required will be the same as the difference in length between long and short sleeves, approximately 30–35 cm.

∴ amount of material required = 1·4 m + 35 cm = 1·75 m.

∴ amount purchased is 1·8 m.

Estimating Amount for Dresses

Bodice

Amount as for blouses—(2 × tuck-in/overlap allowed), i.e.

     long-sleeved: $1 \cdot 8$ m—$(2 \times 15$ cm$) = 1 \cdot 8$ m—30 cm $= 1 \cdot 5$ m.

     short-sleeved: $1 \cdot 4$ m—$(2 \times 15$ cm$) = 1 \cdot 4$ m—30 cm $= 1 \cdot 1$ m.

Skirt

    1 *Straight skirt gathered at waist or slightly flared and fitted at waist line*

Amount required depends on the number of widths of fabric to be used in the skirt.

    a Measure length of skirt and add 7–10 cm for waist turning and hem, e.g. say 70 cm to the knee (to be adjusted above or up to 10 cm below according to fashion) = 80 cm.

    b Multiply this length by the number of widths required (usually 2): 80 cm × 2 = 160 cm = 1·6 m.

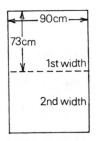

    2 *Gored skirt*

Where the straight edge of the fabric goes to a seam the gores can be dove-tailed several centimetres at their narrow ends. Therefore, to estimate the approximate length required, measure the length of the finished skirt and multiply by 4, e.g.

    70 cm × 4 = 280 cm (2·8 m).

The amount of the overlap will provide turning and hem allowance as well as width for fullness.

    ∴ length purchased = 2·8 m.

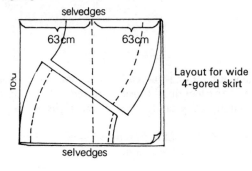

Layout for wide 4-gored skirt

Where the gores have the straight of the fabric running down to the middle of them they can be arranged alternatively with a narrow end to a wide one and vice versa.

For a skirt with 4 gores and a hem circumference of about 2 metres, 2 gores may be placed side by side on double fabric.

∴ length required $= 2 \times$ required length of skirt $+$ hem and seam allowance, e.g.

$2 \times (70 \text{ cm} + 10 \text{ cm}) = 160 \text{ cm} = 1 \cdot 6 \text{ m}$.

∴ length purchased $= 1 \cdot 6 \text{ m}$.

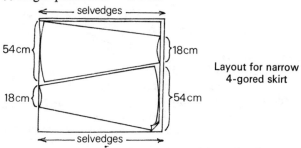

Layout for narrow
4-gored skirt

For a greater number of gores in a wider skirt the pattern pieces are overlapped for less than their complete length and more fabric will be required. This example assumes an overlap of 20 cm and requires:

$2 \times [(2 \times 80, \text{ i.e. } 70 \text{ cm} + 10 \text{ cm hem and seam allowance})$
$- 20 \text{ cm}] = 2 \times 140 \text{ cm} = 280 \text{ cm} = 2 \cdot 8 \text{ m}$.

∴ length purchased $= 2 \cdot 8 \text{ m}$.

Note: Gores cannot be cut in any one of the above ways from any fabric which has a one-way pattern or nap.

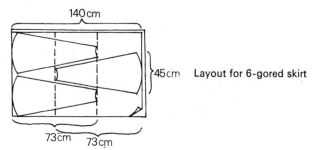

Layout for 6-gored skirt

3 *Circular skirt*

The amount required for each half of a circular skirt is roughly $(2 \times$ skirt length)$+$turnings$+(2 \times \frac{1}{6}$ waist measurement, i.e. $\frac{1}{3}$ waist measurement). The last measurement is based on the fact that the circumference of a circle equals $2\pi r$ or roughly $2 \times 3 \times r$ or $3 \times$ diameter, therefore if the complete circle of the waist is to be 60 cm the diameter must be 20 cm.

∴ length required for half of skirt = $(2 \times 70$ cm$) + 5$ cm $+$ $(2 \times 10$ cm$) = 140$ cm $+ 5$ cm $+ 20$ cm $= 165$ cm.

∴ amount required for full circle of skirt $= 165$ cm $\times 2 = 3 \cdot 3$ m.

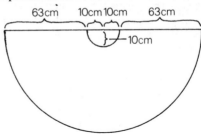

Lengths Required for Dresses

Short-sleeved dress: bodice and sleeves 110 cm
full, gored skirt 280 cm } 390 cm = 3·9 m

Long-sleeved dress: bodice and sleeves 150 cm
full, gored skirt 280 cm } 430 cm = 4·3 m

Short-sleeved dress with circular skirt: 110 cm + 380 cm = 440 cm = 4·4 m

Long-sleeved dress with circular skirt: 150 cm + 330 cm = 480 cm = 4·8 m

Above amounts are for 90 cm wide fabric. 140 cm fabric allows 50 cm extra on each metre.

∴ 1·4 m of 90 cm fabric $\equiv$ 0·9 m of 140 cm fabric.

Lengths Required for Various Garments

Blouse or tunic	Long-sleeved	1·8 m
	Short-sleeved	1·4 m
Dress	Long-sleeved, flared skirt	3·1 m
	Short-sleeved, full gored skirt	3·9 m
Pyjamas	Jacket as for long-sleeved blouse 1·8 m }	4·1 m
	Trousers (2 × length) 2·3 m }	
Nightdress	Sleeveless [97·5 cm + (2 × skirt length)]	3·5 m
	Short-sleeved [97·5 cm + 15 cm + (2 × skirt length)]	3·7 m
	Long-sleeved [97·5 cm + 50 cm + (2 × skirt length)]	4·0 m
Skirt	Gathered (2 widths)	1·6 m
	Gored (wide, full)	2·8 m
	(flared)	1·6 m
	(narrow, full)	2·8 m
	Circular	3·3 m
	Full length (straight)	2·5 m
	(flared)	5·0 m

(Amounts are given for 87–92 cm bust sizes and 90 cm wide fabric.)

USING COMMERCIAL PATTERNS

CHOICE OF STYLE

1 The choice of a flattering style is as important as, if not more than, the choice of a suitable material. As when choosing fabrics, it is essential to know the shortcomings and the assets of one's own figure, and of one's personality. It is well to choose the type of garments in which one feels most at home—to feel one's best is very often to look one's best! The most important consideration is the occasion on which the garments are to be worn, e.g. school or business, leisure, active sports, party wear, beach wear, lingerie.

Figure faults must, however, be carefully examined and styles should be chosen which will disguise them; on the other hand special assets (e.g. slender waist, long back) may be shown off to advantage.

The following table shows common figure faults and how they may be disguised.

Type of Figure	Avoid	Make Use of
Short, full figure	Frills, full sleeves, gathered skirts, wide belts, horizontal stripes	Princess lines, fitted sleeves, gored skirts, French dart
Tall, thin figure	Princess lines, straight skirts, tight-fitting bodices	Gauged, draped effects, gathered skirts, wide belts, good neck interest
Large bust	Draped bodices, frills, high necklines giving unbroken bodice lines, full sleeves	Tailored style of bodices, long revers, fitted sleeves, skirt interest, French dart
Flat chest	Wide necklines, fitted bodices	Draped, gathered styles—proportionately more fullness in bodice than skirt
Thick waist	Wide belts, cummerbund effects, narrow skirts	Narrow belts, fully gored but not gathered skirts, tapering lines on bodice
Large hips	Closely-fitted skirts, hip pockets, narrow bodices	Skirt shaping from waist (gathers only if waist is small), wide neck and shoulder lines to avoid 'triangular' effects, French dart
Short neck	Polo necks or tie-neckbands, wide shoulder-lines	Long V-shaped necklines, open, tailored collars, narrow mandarin necklines, narrow shoulder-lines
Thick/thin upper arms	Cut-away armholes, short sleeves	Well-fitting sleeveless armholes, bracelet and full-length sleeves
Thin neck and shoulders	Wide or low necklines	Mandarin collars, V-shaped necklines, tie-collars, horse-shoe necklines

Note: A classic, well-fitting, uncluttered style with simple neckline, full-length sleeves, semi-fitted waistline and slightly flared skirt, made up in a good quality material, is flattering to all figures.

2 The style chosen should be suitable for the occasions on which the garment will be worn—a coat to be worn over a suit or bulky dress should not be fitted closely. Whatever the occasion a simple, well-made garment is preferable to a more intricate, badly made one.

3 If the material has already been bought the style should be chosen to suit the fabric. The suggestions given on the pattern envelopes should be considered.

4 The style should be well within the capability of the worker to carry out, i.e. a simple, straightforward one to begin with. A plain, well-made dress with a good finish and a comfortable fit is infinitely more attractive than a more ambitious but badly fitting and carelessly sewn suit.

5 Most patterns give at least two alternative versions (e.g. a dress with or without pleats; blouse with or without collar; beach robe with or without hood). Having decided which style is preferred, no further alteration should be made. A good deal of experience is necessary before any major modifications in style can be successfully carried out.

6 Choose the correct pattern size according to the personal measurements noted.

CHOICE OF SIZE

1 Commercial patterns are now made in sizes to suit most figures, from childhood through adolescent development to maturity. Various combinations of measurements are given specific numbers which may be used when ordering patterns, e.g.

Pattern Size	Bust	Waist	Hip	Back Waist Length
Misses' 12	87 cm	67 cm	92 cm	41·5 cm
14	92 cm	71 cm	97 cm	42 cm
Half-size 10½	84 cm	69 cm	89 cm	38 cm
12½	89 cm	74 cm	94 cm	39 cm

2 All patterns are made in proportion to the bust size so, even if waist and hip measurements do not correspond to one's own measurements, the pattern should be bought according to the bust size. Alterations can usually be made very easily in skirt fittings but alterations

made in a bodice involve further alterations in sleeve and collar fittings. Patterns for skirts, jeans and shorts should be chosen according to the hip size, as it is easier to make adjustment to the waist by enlarging or reducing the darts.

3 There are now available two types of paper pattern:

a printed, in which all cutting and fitting lines are printed clearly, with written instructions

b perforated, in which all important markings are indicated by holes in various sizes and arrangements.

For the beginner, a printed pattern is the easier to follow, although a good perforated pattern will provide a key which can be applied very satisfactorily.

Patterns vary considerably in price, depending on the quality and exclusiveness of the styles and on the detail and clarity of the accompanying direction-sheet. There are several makes of good patterns on the market and, unless very experienced, most home dressmakers would be advised to use these. The perforated types give few cutting indications and very short instructions which presuppose a fair amount of knowledge on the part of the worker, while the more elaborate, exclusive patterns involve processes and fitting often outside the capability of any but skilled needlewomen.

PATTERN MARKINGS

Although they vary very slightly according to the manufacturer, most pattern markings are similar, especially the more important ones.

Standard markings for the following features should be learned by heart so that they can be recognized easily on any pattern:

a straight grain of fabric

b place to fold

c darts

d notches showing matching edges

e seam allowance.

Markings showing the position of tucks, gathering, pleats, buttonholes and pockets will appear on a pattern according to its style, but these can be identified easily from the directions included.

Straight Grain of Fabric

This is the most important marking on any piece of pattern. The grain is the direction of the straight threads of the material, either the warp or weft, and unless these threads hang in the correct position the whole line and fit of the garment will be thrown out by the uneven stretching of bias-cut threads. On most portions of garments the warp or selvedge threads, being the stronger, run downwards, therefore the direction 'place to straight grain of material' usually refers to warp threads.

Markings and Meanings

Printed Patterns	Perforated Patterns	Meaning
Long black arrow	Three large holes evenly spaced	Place to straight grain of fabric
Arrow with curved ends	Two small holes Three small holes Oblong slot	Place to fold
Black spots in a triangle with connecting line	Five, seven or nine holes in a triangle	Dart, centre line shows fold of dart
Black diamonds along cutting lines	Edge notched once, twice or three times	Matching edges
Broken line	Row of small, evenly-spaced holes	Hem or seam allowance, usually 1·5 cm from edge

PREPARATION OF PATTERN FOR CUTTING OUT

1 Decide which variation of the pattern style is to be used and sort out the pieces necessary. Refold those pieces not required and replace them in the envelope. Check the pattern pieces against the key given on the back of the envelope and make sure that every piece is there.

2 Iron the pattern with a warm iron if it is too creased to lie flat.

3 Pin pattern pieces together and try against the figure if possible. If this is not practicable, measure pieces carefully and compare them with the measurements required, remembering that each piece has a certain allowance for ease in movement and for wearing over other clothes, e.g.

7·5 cm allowed on complete bust measurement,

5·0 cm allowed on complete waist measurement,

7·5 cm allowed on complete hip measurement.

4 Make any necessary alterations in the pattern.

ALTERING PATTERNS

Although the pattern as it is will fit a well proportioned figure with almost no alteration, allowance sometimes has to be made for differences of shape, e.g. waist smaller than normal for bust and hip measurements, back longer than average in proportion to bust size, length from shoulder to waist not in proportion to length from waist to hem.

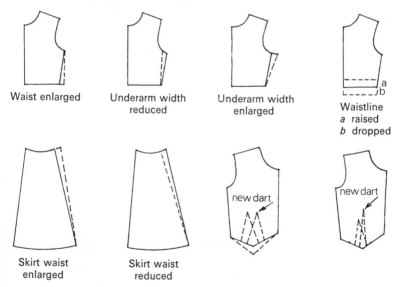

Waist enlarged

Underarm width reduced

Underarm width enlarged

Waistline
a raised
b dropped

Skirt waist enlarged

Skirt waist reduced

new dart

new dart

Note: Remember that 1 cm alteration on each piece of a 4-piece skirt and at both sides of a bodice means a total difference of 4 cm.

All small alterations (maximum 1·5 cm) can be made on seam and hem lines.

For more extensive enlarging and reducing of pattern sizes, however, it is necessary to distribute the alteration evenly through the pattern shape, as follows:

To reduce width   *To reduce length*

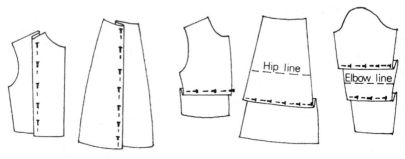

Pleats are pinned into the pattern, each one of a depth equal to ½ of the required amount of reduction.

To increase width

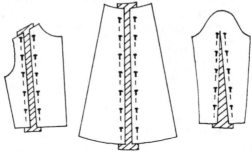

To increase width and length of pattern pieces cut through them at positions shown, place strips of paper behind the cut edges and spread them the required amount.

To increase length

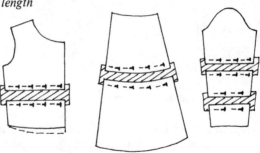

PREPARATION OF MATERIAL FOR CUTTING OUT

1 Straighten the ends of the length of material. Some materials will not tear easily, however—some will 'pull' along the torn edge and some are pulled on to the bias when torn so that the material will not fold in half satisfactorily. In cases like these, cut along a straight thread of the pattern of the material (if the pattern is woven—few printed patterns are true to a thread) or draw out a thread across the end of the fabric and cut along it. To avoid these difficulties, check when buying the material that the assistant tears or cuts it off straight to the grain.

2 If it is not possible to cut out the fabric immediately, remove it from its bag and store it rolled onto a rod or folded paper. It is difficult to lay out badly-creased material.

3 Examine the fabric for flaws. On most lengths of material any bad flaws are indicated on the selvedges opposite with a small tag. Any other faults should be marked with tailor's chalk on the wrong side and great care must be taken when placing the pattern on the material that these flaws are not in conspicuous positions.

4 Test woollens for shrinkage. If not guaranteed shrink-proof, they should be pressed all over evenly with a hot iron over a damp cloth. This will prevent drastic shrinkage when cleaned.

5 Examine the pattern of the material. On any but perfectly plain fabrics great attention must be paid to the pattern to see whether it has an up-and-down motif, a one-way design, a reversible stripe, etc.

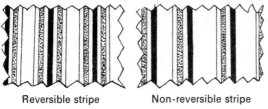

Reversible stripe   Non-reversible stripe

LAYING OUT PATTERN PIECES

1 Follow the diagram of the lay-out of pattern pieces given with the pattern as far as possible, paying particular attention to

   a the direction of the straight threads of the material

   b the need to place to a fold pieces which should not have a seam.
Lay out pieces roughly first to make sure that there is sufficient material.

2 Generally speaking, place pattern pieces with their widest ends at the ends of the length of fabric and place narrower parts end to end so that surplus material is in as few pieces as possible.

3 Insert pins (*inside* the margin of printed patterns) at intervals along all straight edges and diagonally into each corner. Keep the material flat on the table while pinning so that the pattern does not slip out of position.

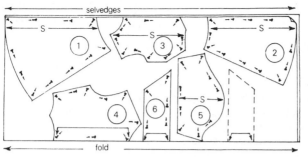

General layout for reversible material

1 Skirt front
2 Skirt back
3 Bodice front
4 Bodice back
5 Sleeve
6 Collar

Layouts for one-way material

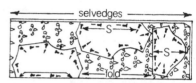

Material folded in half lengthwise has pattern running in the same direction on both thicknesses.

If the material were folded widthwise, the pattern would be reversed on the under layer, therefore the required length must be cut off and laid over a similar length with the pattern running in the same direction on both pieces. Care must be taken that right or wrong sides face each other. Note the extra material required in this instance.

ARRANGING CHECKS AND STRIPES

A well-cut striped or checked dress can look most attractive but a badly-cut one is never effective. A good deal of skill and a great deal of patience are essential for the correct and accurate arrangement of the lines of the design.

Stripes or checks on bodices must meet at:

a shoulder seams

b underarm

c centre front and centre back.

Shoulder seams

The notches must be placed on the same part of the check so that, when made up, the pattern follows from the front over the shoulder to the back.

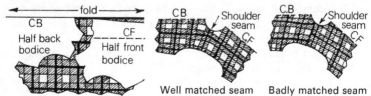

Layout showing notches at same position on neighbouring checks

Well matched seam

Badly matched seam

Underarm seam

The front and back portions of the bodice must have the pattern running uninterrupted round them as well as over the shoulders.

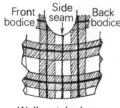

Well matched seam   Badly matched seam   Matching darted seam

If there is an underarm dart in the bodice front the pattern must match between the dart and the waist.

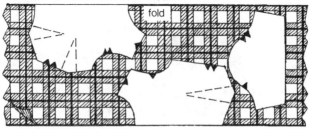

Sleeves

Stripes and checks on bodice must be in line with those on the sleeve, and those running downwards on the sleeve well balanced.

Notches on bodice armhole must correspond in position to those on the sleeve head.

Bodice and sleeve
pattern matching         Bodice and sleeve
pattern not matching

Centre front and centre back

The main line of the fabric pattern should run down the centre front and back of the bodice and similar lines should be balanced evenly on each side of the bodice.

To achieve a well balanced arrangement of stripes and checks, fold the material so that the fold lies along the centre of the main line of the check or the middle of the stripe. Check that the lines are lying exactly over each other throughout the rest of the length of material and pin both edges together. Place centre back to the fold and centre front to a corresponding line.

Well arranged stripes   Badly arranged stripes

Stripes and checks on skirts must meet each other at all seams, forming either straight lines or chevrons.

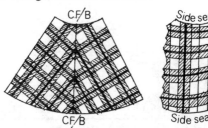

Matching seams can be achieved, again, by laying out the pattern with corresponding notches on similar sections of the design.

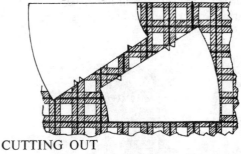

Layout showing position
of corresponding notches

CUTTING OUT

1 Check carefully that all pattern pieces are laid out on the material and that room has been left for any pieces which are to be duplicated. e.g. collars, cuffs, pockets.

2 Cut out all pieces, cutting through the thick black outlines or cutting lines on printed patterns.

Use large, even strokes for cutting, keeping the underneath blade of the scissors and the material on the table at all times, and cutting round the notches.

Cut away from or parallel to yourself, never towards yourself.

3 Lay aside cut-out portions neatly, fold together all reasonably sized cuttings of material and throw away small snippings of material and margins of printed patterns.

4 Transfer all necessary markings from the pattern to the fabric.

TRANSFERRING MARKINGS

1 *Thread marking*

Work thread marking or tailor's tacks through the pattern and both thicknesses of material, using tacking cotton.

If there are several different indications on one piece of pattern (e.g. on a blouse front there may be marks showing seam allowances, notches, darts, tucks, buttonholes and pocket position) work each set with a different colour to make them easy to distinguish when making up the garment.

Work a line of tacking stitches to show positions of centre front and centre back.

Bodice front marked with tailor's tacks

Note: Direction of straight-grain-of-fabric marking and that indicating position of fold need not be transferred from the pattern to the material. After some experience the marks indicating the seam allowance (sometimes referred to as the 'fitting line') may be omitted providing that the width of the turnings allowed is known; or the allowance may be marked merely at the beginning and the end of each seam.

2 *Using carbon paper*

a Place a piece of carbon paper, shiny side downwards to wrong side of fabric, between the pattern and the material.

b Place a second piece, shiny side upwards, underneath both layers of material. Repin the pattern into position.

c Using a ruler as a guide for straight lines, press a tracing wheel over the pattern-markings.

d Remove the pattern.

Using this method, care must be taken to:

(*i*) protect the table surface with a sheet of cardboard.

(*ii*) use yellow or white carbon paper only, as some of the stronger colours will show through to the right side.

(*iii*) place the shiny sides of the carbon paper to the *wrong* sides of the fabric; this marking will wash out but will not rub off, so it should not be worked on the right sides in case the darts, etc., have to be let out.

(*iv*) avoid finger-marking caused by pressing the carbon paper with the hand not holding the tracing wheel.

ORDER OF WORK

1 Choose style.
2 Choose material.
3 Prepare pattern.
4 Prepare material.
5 Lay out pattern on material.
6 Cut out pattern sections.
7 Transfer pattern markings.
8 Separate garment sections.
9 Proceed according to work-sheet instructions.

ADAPTING PATTERN STYLES

Major adaptations of styles should not be attempted by other than expert needlewomen, but it is a relatively simple operation to introduce fullness where required and also to cut yokes into back and front bodice sections.

Introducing Fullness (e.g. tucking blouse front—each tuck to be 1 cm deep.
If each side of tuck is to measure 1 cm, a total of 2 cm must be added to the width of the bodice for every tuck required. The example shows the insertion of three tucks at either side of the C.F.

Original style   Required design

1 Draw round original pattern portion on paper.
2 Cut it out.
3 Mark line of first tuck and cut down marked line.
4 Pin or stick each cut edge to a strip of paper, leaving 2 cm in between.
5 Repeat for lines of second and third tucks.
6 Fold tucks in finished direction and re-cut the neckline.
7 Flatten out and cut out revised pattern.

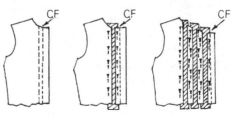

Introducing Pleats

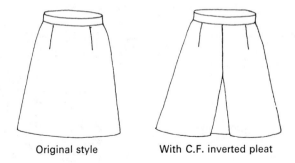

Original style   With C.F. inverted pleat

1 Draw round a basic, slightly flared, skirt pattern.

2 To insert C.F. pleat add a 10 cm extension parallel to the existing C.F. line, as shown.

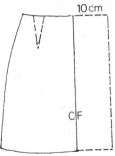

3 Repeat for back of skirt if required.

To insert a knife pleat at each side of inverted pleat:

a Draw a line parallel to C.F. in the required position.

b Cut through the pattern and insert a 10 cm wide strip of paper.

c Fold pleats in required direction and re-cut waist and hem lines.

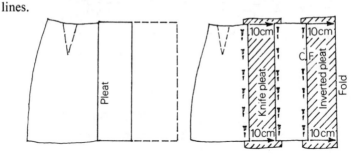

MAKING UP GARMENTS

METHOD FOR SIMPLE DRESS

1 Tack gathers, darts or tucks.

2 Tack up complete garment, without set-in sleeves or collar, and try on. Fit and carry out any necessary alterations. (See *Fitting*, p. 119.)

3 Pin in any alterations required on the right half of the body only. Mark the revised stitching lines with pins, accurately and firmly. Take the sections of the garment apart and transfer the new lines to the opposite side of the garment (using tailor's tacks). Re-tack the whole garment and try on again.

4 Take apart except for darts, tucks or gathers. Work these. Remove tackings and press.

5 Tack shoulder and side seams.

6 Stitch seams and neaten. Press.

7 Machine skirt sections together, neaten seams and press.

8 Tack bodice to skirt.

9 Work waist seam and neaten. Press.

10 Work front or back opening.

11 Make and attach collar.

12 Tack and work seams in sleeves. Press.

13 Tack in sleeves and try on dress. Make any necessary alterations. (See *Fitting*, p. 119.)

14 Check sleeve and hem lengths.

15 Neaten lower edge of sleeve. Press.

16 Stitch in sleeves. Neaten armhole seams and press.

17 Fix bottom hem. Press.

18 Work fastenings.

29 Make belt.

20 Give final pressing.

Special Points to Notice

    1 Tack and stitch with the grain of the seam (run the fingers down the cut edge to test for direction).

    2 Remove tackings and thread markings as soon as they are no longer required.

    3 Fasten off ends of each piece of machine-stitching worked before proceeding to the next one.

    4 As soon as the bodice section is assembled, place it on a hanger and hang it in a cupboard between each session of working.

    5 Allow fully-flared skirts to hang as long as possible before the bottom hem is fixed in order that the bias threads may stretch and the hemline drop. This will avoid the need to re-level the hem later.

Pressing

    6 Try the iron on an odd scrap of the same material before pressing large areas of the garment.

    7 Press with the straight grain of the fabric, never on the bias, which would stretch under the weight of the iron.

    8 Use a damp cloth for springy material and place paper between the garment and the seam turnings to prevent marking.

    9 Press on the wrong side of any material with a matt surface or raised pattern.

    10 Press darts towards each other, either towards centre front or centre back. On thick materials cut the dart open and press flat (see p. 74).

    11 Press French seams towards the back of the garment.

    12 Press gathers by pushing the point of the iron into the gathers.

    13 Use a sleeve board to press sleeve seams and an ironing board for the rest of the garment.

    14 Do not press over fastenings.

FITTING

As has already been stated, each section of the garment should be tried on after it has been tacked together and before it is stitched. Alterations should then be made and the garment re-fitted before any stitching is worked.

    Note that one alteration may lead to another.

Points to Look for When Fitting

Note: Openings should always be pinned together accurately before checking fitting points.

Neck

Check size and depth of neckline and position of shoulder seam at neck point.

    1 If neckline is tight, pulled or wrinkled, it may require lowering.

2 If the shoulder seams slant forward or backward, adjustment is required.

3 If the neckline is too wide or too loose, it requires lifting at the neck point.

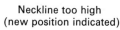

Neckline too high
(new position indicated)

Shoulder line too far back
(new position indicated)

Neckline too loose
(new position indicated)

Bust

Check that length and position of bust darts coincides with bust fullness. Shorten, lengthen or alter position if necessary.

Bust dart too high
(new position indicated)

Bust dart too low
(new position indicated)

Waist

1 Lengthen or shorten darts to coincide with fullness of seat at back and prominence of hip bone at front.

2 Move dart sideways to coincide with fullness of seat or stomach if necessary.

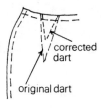

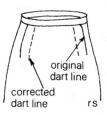

Sleeves

1 If sleeve hangs in folds down the front, due to sleeve being set too far forward, lift sleeve over shoulder towards the back.

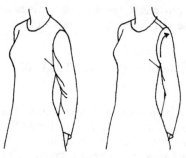

Arrow shows direction in which fullness at sleeve-head must be lifted

2 Wrinkles at back of sleeve, due to sleeve being set too far towards the back of the armhole, can be remedied by lifting the head of the sleeve over the shoulder towards the front.

Arrow shows direction in which head of sleeve must be lifted in order to get rid of creases

3 If shoulder is too long, causing sleeve to drop, shorten the seam at the shoulder point and re-shape armhole.

Note: Many fitting alterations can be avoided if the correct size of pattern is purchased and necessary alterations carried out before cutting.

E

DRESSMAKING TERMS

Most expressions used in garment-making explain themselves and need no further comment. There are, however, a few terms occurring in instructions which may not be obvious to the beginner. It is essential to understand the meaning of these and short explanations are given below.

Grain
The direction of the threads in weaving. (See pp. 50 and 107.)

Balance Marks
These are the marks on paper patterns (notches or black diamonds) which show exactly where two sections of a garment should be joined. They are important because by using them, stretching of one edge more that another is avoided and the garment will hang correctly. The marking must be transferred to the fabric before the pattern is removed. They also show the position of fullness (e.g., where gathering is to be commenced and finished), and position of pockets, etc.

By transferring markings through two thicknesses of material both sides can be made identical.

Gusset
A shaped section introduced into garments at the junctions of seams to allow freedom of movement by providing extra room, e.g. underarm of kimono/magyar sleeve.

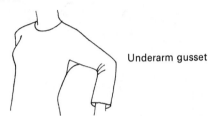

Underarm gusset

Zip Openings
Openings in garments which are closed by semi-concealed, concealed, visible or invisible zip fasteners.

Fitting Lines

The lines on which stitching is to be worked, i.e. those indicating the seam allowance. (See p. 108.)

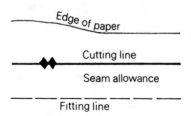

Cut-away Armhole

This style results in a very narrow shoulder and needs an all-in-one neck and armhole facing.

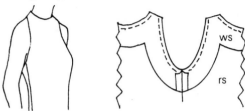

Fitted Sleeve

A full-length sleeve set smoothly into the armhole, with darts shaping the elbow. Sometimes cut in two pieces, when no darts are necessary, as the shaped seams provide the fitting.

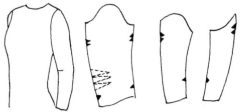

Three-quarter Sleeve

A sleeve reaching to just below the elbow. It may be gathered or fitted.

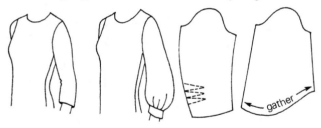

Bishop Sleeve

A long, full sleeve gathered into the armhole and wristband.

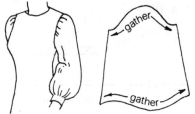

Raglan Sleeve

A sleeve cut in two sections, the upper part of each forming the shoulder section of the bodice. The sleeve should be completed before setting into the bodice.

Magyar/Kimono Sleeve

A sleeve cut in one with bodice sections. The seam must be snipped at curve to avoid puckering. The underarm seam must be strengthened to prevent splitting. Ideally, these styles should have a gusset.

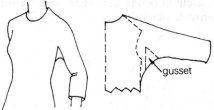

Dolman Sleeve

Similar shape to magyar sleeve (cut in one with the bodice), but closer fitting at the wrist and fuller in the underarm, as the allowance for movement (provided in the magyar sleeve by the gusset) is built into the pattern.

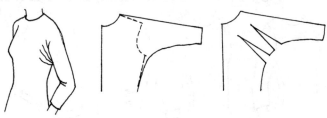

Puff Sleeve

A short, fully gathered sleeve, usually used for children's garments.

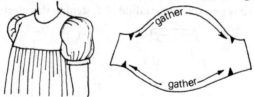

A-line Skirt

A slightly flared skirt with sufficient width for walking; it may be mini, midi or maxi-length.

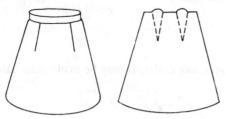

Shape of skirt section

Gored Skirt

A skirt cut in several sections, fitting closely at waist and flaring out from hips.

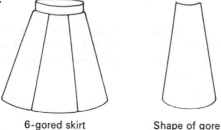

6-gored skirt   Shape of gore

Panelled Skirt

Similar to gored skirt but less full, sections being shaped to fit the figure. There is usually no side seam and the fitting over the hips is provided by side darts (sometimes called the 'matchbox skirt').

opening

Shape of panels

Wrapover Skirt

A skirt which fastens with a double width wrapover at the front or the back. Velcro is an excellent method of fastening this skirt.

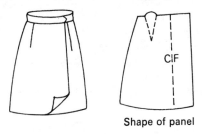

Shape of panel

Peter Pan Collar

A flat, rounded, one-piece collar. It may be made detachable.

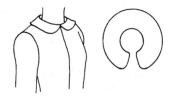

Shirt Collar

A straight, turned-over collar which may also be worn open as a collar and revers if required. The fronts of the bodice are faced so that they may be turned back. Blouses and pyjamas are often made so that collar may be worn open or closed.

Wing Collar

Collar cut in one with fronts of bodice and faced with the front facings.

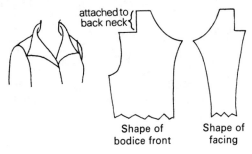

Shape of
bodice front

Shape of
facing

Polo Collar

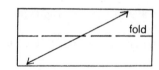

Mandarin Collar

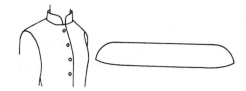

DRESSMAKING METHODS

ATTACHING COLLARS

Collars with Faced Revers

   1 Mark centre of inner edge of collar.

   2 Pin centre of collar neck edge to centre back of bodice and at matching notches.

   3 Tack from centre of neck edge to front of neck edge, matching notches.

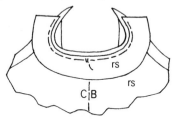

   4 Fold facing extension back or place separate facing over front and collar. Tack into position. (Edge of facing should have been neatened previously.)

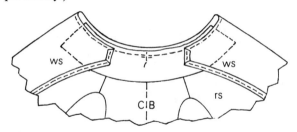

5 Cut a crossway strip long enough to reach from facing edge to facing edge+2·5 cm.

6 Tack over collar, right sides facing, overlapping facing equally at each end.

Stitch from one end of the neck edge to the other.

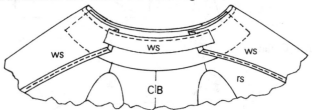

7 Snip neck edge at intervals to allow curved seam to spread.

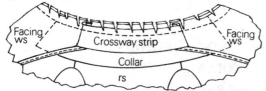

8 Turn facings to wrong side and tack along seamed line, continuing along the turned crossway facing.

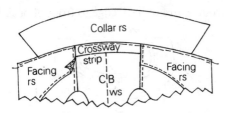

9 Turn under the raw edge of the crossway strip, tack it to the garment and hem into position. Hem the turned edge of the facing to the shoulder seam. This method is suitable for Peter Pan and Eton collars.

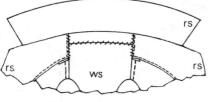

Completed collar facing

Mandarin or Polo Collars

1 Stitch and turn out ends of collar as far as neck-edge fitting line.

2 Attach underside of collar to neck edge of garment with right sides facing and matching C.F., C.B. and shoulder marks. Tack and machine.

3 Trim, clip and layer turnings, pressing towards the collar.

4 Turn under the raw edge of the top collar, tack and hem.

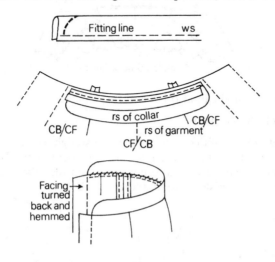

Straight Collars

1 Pin on collar and facings as previously shown.

2 Tack from shoulder seams to front openings as before.

3 Tack on under section only of back collar.

4 Stitch in three sections as tacked, making sure that stitching lines join into one continuous row.

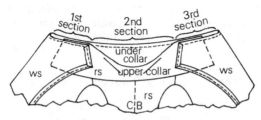

5 Turn facings to wrong side of garment (snip turnings first).

6 Turn under raw edge of upper collar and tack folded edge just above stitching line.

7 Hem upper collar to neck edge turning.

For collars similar to above, where there is no facing, attach complete collar as back neck above.

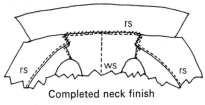

Completed neck finish

Note: This method can also be used for mandarin and tie collars.

SETTING IN SLEEVES

The secret of a well-fitted sleeve is that the straight of the material runs down the middle of the sleeve from the shoulder (see p. 121), therefore it is essential to place the pattern correctly on the fabric and to mark balance notches on sleeve-head and on armhole.

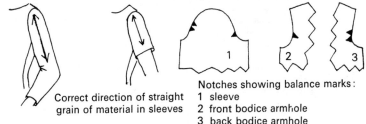

Correct direction of straight grain of material in sleeves

Notches showing balance marks:
1 sleeve
2 front bodice armhole
3 back bodice armhole

1 Join underarm seam of sleeve. Press and neaten.

2 Fold sleeve flat with seam opposite middle of sleeve.

3 Gather round head of sleeve from fold to fold. Work one row on fitting line and one 6 mm nearer to the raw edge.

4 Place sleeve inside armhole, right sides facing. Pin at balance marks and seams. Arrange fullness inside top of armhole, arranging gathers evenly or easing regularly. Pin at regular intervals from the sleeve side.

5 From the sleeve side tack along fitting line, starting from where gathers begin and working ungathered portion first.

6 Try on and adjust if necessary.

7 When correctly placed, stitch along fitting line from sleeve side. (Ease the material under the machine foot to avoid stitching in tiny pleats.) Fasten off ends securely from sleeve side of stitching.

8 First press the line of stitching flat on the w.s. From the right side, working over a pad on the end of the sleeve board, press the turnings into the sleeve-head.

Note: Use a pressing cloth for all materials. Do not overpress fabrics that are liable to stretch.

9 Trim turnings to 1·3 cm.

10 Neaten by one of the following methods:

a machine zig-zag

b 3-step zig-zag

c mock French seam.

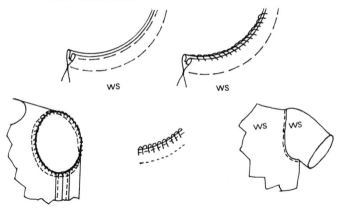

Completed armhole   Sleeve seam finish   Armhole showing completed French seam

(*i*) Turn in the raw edges of the sleeve and the bodice over 6 mm towards each other.

(*ii*) Oversew or machine into position. When finished the raw edges are completely enclosed and the seam should resemble a French seam. This is suitable for fine, washable fabrics.

d binding

(*i*) Place right side of crossway strip to garment side of armhole, raw edges together.

Tack 6 mm from edge of turning to within 2·5 cm each side of seam, leaving 3·8 cm of crossway strip overlapping.

Make a proper crossway-join (see p. 52) so that joined strip fits armhole. Press. Complete tacking.

(*ii*) Stitch immediately under the tacking from strip side. Remove tackings.

(*iii*) Turn crossway strip to sleeve side of armhole, turn under raw edge and tack just above the machine-stitching. Hem into position, taking care that stitches do not go through to right side.

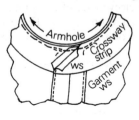

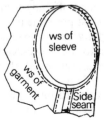

Joining of crossway strip   Completed armhole binding

e French seam

On very thin materials which fray easily and are too transparent for a binding to be satisfactory, French seams may be worked. (See p. 20.)

FINISHING EDGES OF SLEEVES

Short Sleeves
Bound: See p. 54.
Faced: See pp. 55, 62.
Scalloped: See pp. 59, 155.
Cuffed: The cuffs may be attached
in similar ways to the collars by:

a applying a crossway strip as a facing

b machining the under cuff to the sleeve edge and hemming the upper cuff to the turning.

Note: A shaped cuff (see pointed one above) must be tacked round the stitched edge before attaching to sleeve. This prevents the seam from being pulled out of position and becoming visible on the right side of the cuff.

Long Sleeves

Whatever the method chosen to finish off the sleeve edge, the necessary opening should be worked first. (See p. 62.)

Cuffed: Similar methods may be used to those described for short sleeves.

Bound: As for short sleeves.

Faced: As for short sleeves.

Adapted facings: See page 62.

Plain hem finish:

1 Mark line of sleeve edge and cut turning to equal width all round.

2a For woollen materials tack and machine bias binding to edge of turning on the right side. Make a true crossway join in the binding to correspond with the sleeve seam.

b For other materials use machine edge-stitch or zig-zag to neaten raw edge.

3 Turn sleeve turning to wrong side along marked line. Tack along folded edge of sleeve and bottom edge of binding. Slipstitch into position.

4 Edge-stitch wrist-line of sleeve if required.

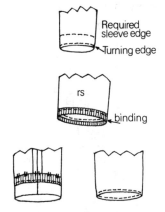

Note: If sleeve becomes considerably narrower at the wrist it may be necessary to slope out the sleeve turning of the part to be turned under in order to fit the wider portion.

SKIRT HEMS

General rules

1 Allow flared skirts or any others with bias-cut panels (particularly circular ones) to hang for as long as possible—at least a week—to allow the weight of the skirt to stretch the bias threads as much as possible before the hem is fixed.

2 Put on the garment and do up any fastenings. Adjust the belt which will be worn and wear appropriate shoes.

3 Stand quite straight and do not look down at the person marking the hemline (the height of the skirt alters as the body bends forward).

4 Have hemline marked with a patent hem-guide or with a metre-stick. When hem-guide is used the chalk line blown on to the material should be marked with pins, as the powdered chalk easily rubs off.

When a metre-stick is used, place it as close to the skirt as possible, with the square end firmly on the floor or table and held perfectly straight. Measure up from the bottom of the rule to the required length and mark the level with pins. Do not disarrange the folds of the skirt any more than necessary.

5 Fold the turning to the wrong side along the pinned line, removing pins and replacing them at right angles to the folded edge.

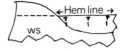

6 Tack along pinned edge. Press edge only (i.e. along fold) after removing pins. Check that corresponding seams in skirt are of equal length.

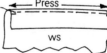

7 Measure off the depth of hem required, i.e. 5 cm for slightly flared or straight skirts, becoming narrower as the fullness of the skirt increases. A full circular skirt will have a maximum hem depth of 6 mm.

8 Arrange fullness of hem by gathering or pleating. Pleats must be evenly placed, at equal distances and facing towards centre front or centre back. Gathers must be evenly distributed.

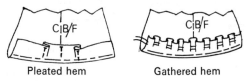

| Pleated hem | Gathered hem |

Note: On woollen materials the fullness of the hem can be shrunk with a hot iron and damp cloth.

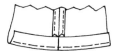

9 Note that seams in turning must lie in line with seams in skirt.
10 Finish hem according to material.

Hems on Cottons and Other Lightweight Materials
First method

1 Dispose of fullness with gathers or small pleats if necessary.
2 Turn under raw edge 6 mm and edge-stitch. Tack hem into position.
3 Turn hem back, away from worker, and slip hem invisibly, taking up one thread of the garment material.

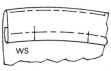

Hem turned and tacked

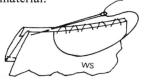

Hem folded back and hemmed invisibly

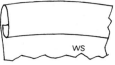

Completed hem

Second method

   1 Gather edge of turning.

   2 Place right side of crossway facing to right side of turning and tack along gathering line. Stitch through turning and facing.

   3 Turn crossway strip up to skirt above hem and tack, folding under the second turning. Invisibly hem into position.

Note: A crossway facing is required, rather than a straight one, because of the curve of the hem.

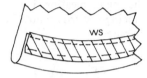 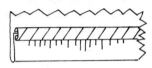

   Either of these methods may also be used without any disposal of fullness in the turning, i.e. on a straight skirt.

Hems on Woollens and Thicker Materials

First method

   1 Apply a crossway strip to the raw edge of the turning as shown.

   2 Turn binding to wrong side of hem and machine or stab stitch into position along the seam.

Note: It is not necessary to turn under the raw edge of the binding, and the stab stitch or machining should be worked into the hem turning only.

   3 Tack hem into position and slip hem as before (see p. 55.)

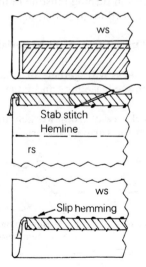

Second method
Herringbone the raw edge to the skirt, taking up the back of the skirt threads only. (For method of working herringbone stitch see p. 16.)

This method is suitable for napped materials which do not fray, e.g. velour cloth, Crimplene and jersey.

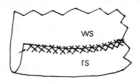

Third method

1 Neaten raw edge of hem with overcasting, zig-zag or 3-step zig-zag according to fabric.

2 Tack hem into position.

3 Fix as shown on p. 136.

Simple Hems
Rolled hem: used on very thin materials. No tacking is required, the hem being rolled between the fingers as it is worked.

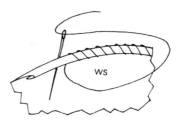

Machined hem: used on straight edges, mainly on the sides of aprons and on household articles. Hems of well-made garments should very seldom be finished in this way. Care must be taken that tacking and machining are worked as closely to the fold of the turning as possible.

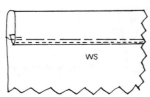

Double hem: used for straight hems on plain transparent materials. Double the normal hem depth should be allowed when cutting out.

  a Turn half of the hem allowance to the wrong side and tack— raw edge will lie on hemline.

  b Fold over on hemline and tack into position.

  c Fix hem with decorative stitching, e.g. pinstitch (see p. 154) or machine embroidery.

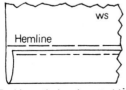

Tacking stitches inserted in first turning

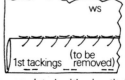

Hem completed with pin stitching (worked from right side of hem)

False hem: useful for lengthening and neatening skirt hems. The false hem strip should be cut to the same shape as the hemline of the garment, with seams matching those of the skirt. It is then applied as a facing, and the upper edge invisibly slip hemmed.

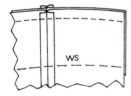

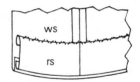

Note line of skirt material brought to wrong side along edge of false hem

WAISTBANDS

Interfaced Cloth Waistband

  1 Cut the waistband long enough to allow the overwrapping end to be cut to a point and the underwrap to extend 2·5–5 cm beyond the edge of the opening.

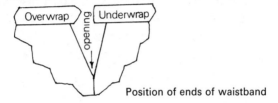

Position of ends of waistband

2 Tack and fix interfacing to wrong side of waistband as shown, placing the inner edge to the fold line and the outer edge to the fitting line.

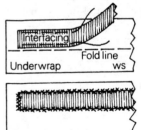

Preparation of waist band I: interfacing tacked to wrong side

Preparation of waist band II: interfacing herringboned to band

3 Place the right side of the waistband to the wrong side of the skirt. Tack and stitch along fitting line.

4 Press waistband upwards from skirt, turn to right side along fold line and tack along the fold, after working the ends as shown.

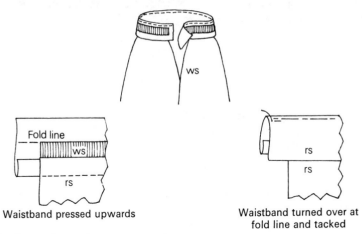

Waistband pressed upwards

Waistband turned over at fold line and tacked

Shaping ends
Pointed end: Turn waistband back along fold line and stitch pointed shape, beginning at the first line of stitching and finishing on the fold.
Snip the turnings as shown by dotted lines. Turn to right side.

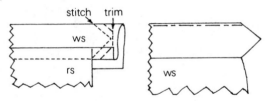

Square end: Turn waistband back as shown. Snip the turning of the waistband at the skirt edge and turn it downwards.

Stitch from fold of waistband down the width of the waistband and across underwrap to meet first line of stitching. Snip turnings as shown by dotted line and turn to right side.

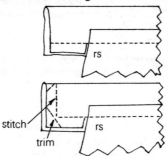

4 Turn under seam allowance on front of waistband and tack just below first row of stitching. Stitch on the edge of the waistband along both long and both short edges.

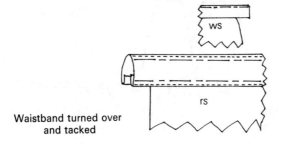

Waistband turned over and tacked

5 Attach fastenings—hook on wrong side of point; worked bar to correspond on underwrap; hooks and eyes to hold underwrap in position.

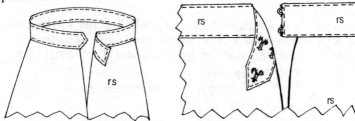

Curved Petersham Waistband

1 Cut petersham to waist measurement $+1\cdot3$ cm–$2\cdot5$ cm for ease $+5$ cm for turnings.

2*a* Turn back $2\cdot5$ cm at each end and oversew edges together. Attach hooks and eyes.

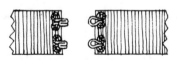

or

b Slot jupe-fix sections onto petersham ends and oversew down.

3 Divide petersham belt into half and mark halfway line. Repeat with each section, marking the quarters. Repeat with skirt waist.

4 Place upper edge of petersham to fitting line of skirt waist, wrong side of petersham to right side of skirt. Match marked quarter sections and pin with pins at right angles to edge. Tack.

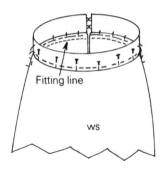

Fitting line

ws

5 Machine along edge of petersham to within $2\cdot5$ cm of placket fastening (usually zip) at each side.

CARE AND USE OF MACHINES

With careful use and regular attention a sewing machine will give efficient service for many years—in fact, there are many family heirlooms still giving excellent results. There are on sale today attractive new machines which may be adjusted to do many of the dressmaking processes which for years have been worked only by hand (fixing bottom hems; sewing on buttons; working buttonholes; embroidering, etc.). These are, however, expensive and should not be regarded as essential for satisfactory craftsmanship.

To give efficient service a sewing machine must be correctly threaded, considerately used and regularly serviced.

GENERAL RULES

1 *Use the correct size of needle and thickness of thread for the material.* For general use a No. 14/80 needle is satisfactory but for extra fine or coarse fabrics the needle should be changed accordingly. (See table on p. 146.) The thread on the reel and on the bobbin must be the same number.

Special needles may be obtained, with very hard points, for use on synthetic fabrics. Needle sizes are being colour-coded for easy recognition and identification.

2 *Thread the machine correctly.* With so many different models in use it is not possible to generalize. It is essential to know the correct method for the machine in question, however, and this can be ascertained from the booklet of instructions provided with the model or bought from a dealer. (In the latter case it is necessary to be able to quote the name and number of the model.)

3 *See that the bobbin is correctly placed.* Again it is not convenient to generalize, but unless the correct method is used for the particular machine satisfactory stitching cannot be obtained.

4 *Bring the bobbin thread through to the top of the machine ready for stitching.* Hold the thread from the needle in the left hand and turn the wheel slowly, bringing the needle down into the hole below. Continue to turn the wheel slowly until the thread being held is pulling up the loop of that from the bobbin. Pull the loop through until the end appears.

5 *Place both ends of thread under the presser foot and pass them towards the back of the machine.*

6 *Make sure that the needle is at its highest point before stitching.* If a reasonable length of thread is left but the needle is down, the needle will become unthreaded as it rises.

7 *Test the stitch on a scrap of the material to be sewn.* The material should be of double thickness and the stitch carefully examined *on both sides.*

8 *Correct the tension if necessary.* (See p. 13.) The tension of the stitch is regulated by the two small tension plates and tension spring. The plates can be made to press more or less firmly against each other by tightening or loosening the screw passing through them. The thread from the reel is passed between them and over the spring and the rate at which it is allowed to slip through them regulates the tension of the stitch.

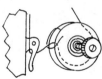

9 *Correct the length of the stitch if necessary.* The stitch can be lengthened or shortened to suit the material by using the stitch regulator. This may be a simple screw which winds clockwise to make the stitch larger, and anti-clockwise to make it smaller, or a gauge which gives a reading showing the number of stitches worked to an inch or the length of each stitch in millimetres. Smaller stitches should be used on fine materials than on thicker ones.

10 *Place the garment to be sewn with the main part to the left of the needle, leaving the space under the arch free.*

11 *Place the inner edge of the presser foot against the edge of the hem or just to the side of the seam line.* Make a habit of using the presser foot as a guide to sewing along folded edges and fitting lines.

12 *Make sure that no pins have been left in hems or seams.* If the machine is worked over these the needle can be broken. In order to stitch over pins with a hinged presser foot, make sure that the pins are placed at right angles to the line of stitching.

13 *Stitch smoothly along tacked lines.* It is essential that tacking is straight and accurate. The machine-stitching should be worked as close to the tacking stitches as possible, inside them rather than outside ('outside' means between the tacking and the raw edges). The machine must be operated without jerking—the handle being turned smoothly or the treadle pressed regularly or the electric control (knee or foot) operated gently.

14 *When turning corners, keep the needle down in the fabric and raise the presser foot; turn the material, replace the presser foot.* Do not raise the presser foot and the needle together until the stitching is completed.

15 *Do not pull the material as it passes under the foot.* Never try to hurry the machine: it will feed the material through without assistance unless it is too thick to be stitched in this way. By pulling it the length of the stitch is altered and the whole timing of the stitching is upset.

16 *When stitching is completed, raise the presser foot,* make sure that the needle is at its highest point, ease out the material from under the foot, and pull both threads very gently towards the back of the machine. Do not pull sharply, as this will bend or break the needle.

GENERAL CARE

1 Never work the machine while it is threaded unless the presser foot is lowered. The interlocking of the two threads will quickly jam the mechanism.

2 Never use the machine while any parts of it are loose. Any loose screws must be tightened immediately. Do not remove the slide plate over the bobbin case—it will slide out quite sufficiently to allow the bobbin to be put into position. Frequent removal of the plate will eventually strain the spring and the plate will not lie flat.

3 Remove all threads, pins and snippings from the machine as they are produced. Trapped in the mechanism these can cause serious dislocation of the machinery.

4 Keep the machine dusted and cover it up when not in use, leaving the presser foot down.

5 Oil the machine according to the maker's instruction book.

6 If the machine is electrically operated make sure that plugs and flexes are in good condition—plugs tightly screwed and flexes un-knotted and showing no bare wires.

SPECIAL CLEANING

1 Disconnect the belt of treadle machines, and the plugs of electric ones.

2 Collect pieces of rag (without loose threads), a small soft brush, screwdriver, oil can (filled with machine oil—use only the special oil supplied for the purpose).

3 Remove the slide plate and the needle.

4 Unscrew the plate covering the teeth under the needle shaft.

5 Brush out all fluff, dust and tiny threads from the mechanism from the top. Turn back the head of the machine and repeat from underneath.

6 Oil the mechanism from all the oil-holes and squeeze a few drops into the bobbin race.

7 Run the machine gently for a few minutes to distribute the oil throughout the mechanism. Leave it standing for a time to let the oil soak well into working parts.

8 Remove all surplus oil.

9 Clean up remainder of machine-head and dust out the space below it.

10 Replace plates and screws, making sure that these and all others are screwed tightly in position. Replace needle.

11 Leave a small piece of absorbent material under the presser foot to catch any oil which may seep through the mechanism.

12 Remember to wipe over the machine carefully and run on a piece of scrap material before using on a garment again. Run the machine for a few minutes before re-threading.

ATTACHMENTS

Use of Attachments
Piping (zipper) foot attachments, darners, hemmers, binders, etc., are often provided as part of the machine equipment. Use them according to instructions. Practise on an odd piece of material before using attachments on garments.

Using Machine for Gathering See p. 71.

Common Faults and Remedies

Fault	Cause	Remedy
Loops on wrong side of stitching	*a* Tension too loose on thread from reel *b* Bobbin upside-down	*a* Tighten tension screw *b* Correct bobbin
Loops on right side of stitching	Reel thread tension too tight	Loosen tension screw
Note: Incorrect threading may account for either of above faults		
Stitches not interlocking	Needle in backwards	Reverse needle
Thread breaking	*a* Tension too tight *b* Incorrect threading *c* Needle blunt or bent *d* Needle size incorrect for the thread used *e* Spool too full and jamming the bobbin race	*a* Loosen tension screw *b* Re-thread correctly *c* Replace needle with new one *d* Replace according to table on p. 146 *e* Remove bobbin and unwind a portion of the thread
Missed stitches	*a* Needle blunt, twisted or too low *b* Material pulled as it is being stitched *c* Thread too thick for the needle used	*a* Replace needle with new one in correct position *b* Use hand to guide, not pull, the work *c* Use identical threads on reel and bobbin
Puckered seams	*a* Tension too tight *b* Needle blunt	*a* Loosen tension screw *b* Replace needle
Broken needle	*a* Presser foot loose so that needle hits it instead of passing between two 'toes' *b* Seam or hem too thick for size of needle *c* Needle loose and striking presser foot *d* Presser foot passing over pins in folds and needle hitting them *e* Needle striking knots in tacking threads	*a* Tighten presser foot screw *b* Cut away some of bulk where not required. Check needle size. Ease material under foot *c* Tighten needle screw *d* Remove all pins before machining *e* Never fasten stitching on or off with knots
Material not moving under presser foot	*a* Too great thickness of fabric *b* Stitch regulator screwed to fullest extent of shortening *c* Beginning stitching too close to edge	*a* Avoid jamming too many folds of fabric under the foot *b* Adjust stitch regulator *c* Correct position of presser foot

General Classification of Needles and Thread

Size of Needle	Material	Thread
9–11 **60–70**	Fine silks, georgette, nylon, muslin and other delicate fabrics	60–100 cotton pure silk Drima Trylko
14 **80**	General domestic fabrics, light woollens, shirtings, heavier silks	50 cotton pure silk 50 Sylko Drima Trylko
16–18 **90–100**	Heavy cottons (denims, etc.), thick wools, suitings	40 cotton 40 Sylko Trylko

FURTHER STUDY

THINGS TO DO

1 Work small sections of each of the following processes: binding edge of short sleeve; facing edge of short sleeve; scalloping edge of short sleeve; applying cuff to short sleeve; facing hem of long sleeve; faced opening at wrist of long sleeve.

Mount each specimen and attach a written sheet answering the following questions:

a What variations of this method could be carried out?

b On which garments could this method be used?

c What other length of sleeve could also be neatened by this method?

d What opening (if any) would be suitable for use with this method of neatening?

e What seam would be used on this sleeve?

Illustrate each set with pictures or drawings of suitable garments.

2 Work small sections of each of the following processes: gathered hem; pleated hem; faced hem; bound hem; whipped hem; false hem.

Mount each specimen with answers to the following:

a On which garments would this hem be used? State the material.

b What makes this hem suitable for its use?

c What are the difficulties in working this hem?

d How can these difficulties be overcome?

Illustrate as suggested above.

3 Work small sections of the following waistband finishes: interfaced cloth waistband; curved petersham waistband.

Mount each specimen with answers to the following:

a On what garments would this method be used? State the material.

b What fastening would be used?

c What opening would be used?

d What methods of reducing fullness round the waist could be used before applying the waistband?

e How would a garment finished in this way be laundered?

Attach samples of petersham and washable belting to the specimen of an interfaced waistband. Illustrate as previously suggested.

4 Find out as much as you can about *a*. the history and *b*. the methods of fabric weaving.

5 Make *one or other* of the following:

a Cut out, fit and make up a blouse requiring

(*i*) a set-in sleeve

(*ii*) an attached collar

(*iii*) some form of reduced fullness

and a skirt, either fully flared or of a simple, fitted style.

b Cut out and make up a beach outfit involving

(*i*) shorts with fitted waistband and opening

(*ii*) an overblouse with faced neckline and armholes.

QUESTIONS TO ANSWER

1 Complete the following statements by filling in the blank spaces with words taken from the right-hand column.

Section A

a .... is a fine semi-transparent cotton fabric which may be used as a dress material or as an interfacing.

b .... is a cotton fabric which has been given a fluffy surface to add warmth in wearing.

c .... is a soft, cotton, plain-weave fabric which has a slight sheen.

d Cotton fabrics used for children's nightwear are given a .... finish to make them non-inflammable.

e In weaving some fabrics a diagonal effect is produced and this is called a .... weave.

f When fabric is woven to give a corded effect by 'floating' the weft threads at regular intervals behind the warp threads, the material is known as ....

g Velvet must be cut in one direction because the .... causes it to shade differently

petersham

pile

piqué

sanforized

organdie

Proban

winceyette

lawn

jersey

when it hangs upwards and downwards.

h Most fibres can be machine-knitted to produce fabric; these are called .... materials.

i .... is a narrow stiffening used as waistbands for skirts.

j When fabric is given a .... finish it has been pre-shrunk in manufacture and no allowance for shrinkage need be made when cutting it.

twill

Section B

a A round, flat collar suitable for children's dresses and for blouses is called a .... collar.

b A straight collar which turns over on itself is a .... collar.

c A sleeve which is full length and gathered both at the wrist and at the shoulder is called a .... sleeve.

d A .... sleeve is cut in one with the bodice and fullness for ease of movement is allowed at the underarm.

e A shaped panel section of a skirt is known as a ....

f In a perforated pattern the marking is ○ ○ ○ ; the equivalent marking on a printed pattern is ....

g On a printed pattern there is a marking ←——→ ; the equivalent marking on a perforated pattern is ....

h Matching edges of pattern pieces of a printed pattern are shown as ....

i A small shaped section inserted into a garment to allow for freedom of movement is called a ....

j The success of machine-stitching in having no loops visible on either the right or wrong side of the fabric depends on the .... of the thread.

gusset

tension

shirt

Peter Pan

bishop

gore

dolman

2*a* State how and where personal measurements should be taken before buying a commercial pattern.

b Using sketches and notes, show how a pattern should be altered for a figure with narrow, sloping shoulders.   (A.E.B.)

3*a* Why is it important to transfer pattern markings from a pattern onto fabric after cutting out the pattern pieces?

b Name *four* ways in which this can be done.

c Describe the method you consider to be best, giving your reasons.   (A.E.B.)

4 What markings would you expect to find on a pattern for a short-sleeved shirt blouse, which fastens at the front with buttons and buttonholes, in order to assist you to make it up? Describe in detail, with the aid of diagrams, a method of transferring these pattern markings to material. (A.E.B.)

5a By three sketches show how striped fabrics can be used to good effect in children's dresses and play clothes.

b What special care is needed when using striped fabrics? (A.E.B.)

6 Sketch the front and back views of a housecoat for yourself which features a pocket and has no waist seam. Suggest suitable material for it. By drawing a layout, estimate the amount of material required. (A.E.B.)

7 Suggest a complete outfit (day and night wear) for a four-year-old girl, illustrating your answer with sketches. Say what materials you would choose for the garment and give your reasons.

8 Sketch and describe a party dress that has some trimming added at the neck and hem. Give, with reasons, your choice of material for the dress and describe the trimming. Give the amount of material and trimming required in metres. Show by diagram(s) how the trimming that you have chosen is attached to the garment. (A.E.B.)

9a Sketch the front and back views of a suitably styled dress for each of the following:

(i) a fabric which is firm and closely-woven

(ii) a fabric which is soft and drapes well

Label the style features clearly.

b Name a fabric which fits each description and which would be suitable for each dress you have designed.

c Choose one dress and give the order of making up after cutting out. (C.U.B.)

10 You are making a sleeveless cardigan in a 5 cm even-checked fabric.

a List the points you would note when:

(i) laying the pattern on the fabric

(ii) joining the side seams of the cardigan to ensure that when the cardigan is completed the checks will match.

b Show by clearly-labelled diagrams how you would make and attach three fabric loops (rouleau loops) at the centre front of the cardigan which is neatened with a shaped facing. (C.U.B.)

11 Sketch an outfit which could be made up in two completely different fabrics and show how the items could be mixed and matched. State the fabric and colour used in each case and show the adaptations you would make to the basic pattern for each garment.

12 What do you understand by 'seam allowance'? How would you cope with the seams of the following parts of garments in order to ensure a good finish?

a the attachment of a Peter Pan collar to a child's Viyella dress

b the neatening of a plain round neck on a cotton dress, using a facing

c the attachment of the gathered skirt of a nylon nightdress to the double yoke.

13 What do you understand by 'the grain of the fabric'? Give as many examples as possible of the importance of grain when cutting out garments.

14*a* Why must a set-in sleeve always be eased into an armhole?

b Where is the ease to be found on the sleeve?

c How would you set a sleeve into an armhole in preparation for machine-stitching?

15 Explain, with the help of diagrams, the differences between:

a a binding and a facing

b tucks and darts

c 'cross-cut' and 'bias'

d a panel and a gore

e plain and twill weave.

16 Give instructions for the general care of the sewing machine. Explain how you would take precautions to ensure a good machine stitch when working on *a*. nylon and *b*. woollen tweed.   (A.E.B.)

17 The sewing maching is an essential piece of equipment for a dressmaker. What points would you consider when buying a new machine? State instances, giving reasons, where

a machining is more suitable than hand-sewing

b hand-sewing is more suitable than machining.   (A.E.B.)

18 Sketch *three* of the following:

a a neckline which would improve the appearance of a person with a short thick neck

b a dress which would improve the appearance of a tall angular figure

c a bodice style which would improve the appearance of a flat-chested figure

d a skirt style which would improve the appearance of a person with large hips.   (C & G)

19 List the information that is required to estimate quantities of material.

How would you make a quick estimate of the material required (two different widths) for a simple dress for an average figure?   (C & G)

20 What are the measurements you should know before buying a commercial pattern for a dress?

Show by diagrams how to:

a lengthen by 2·5 cm a bodice of a dress which has a bust dart and a waist dart

b shorten by 2·5 cm a skirt which is slightly flared.   (A.E.B.)

4

DECORATIVE PROCESSES

Some processes combine a useful purpose with a decorative effect, as has already been shown, for instance tucks, pleats, bindings. It is sometimes desired to introduce decoration for its own sake, however, and it is then important to observe the following rules:

1 No garment which is not well made should ever be decorated.

2 The method of decoration used should be suitable for the material, the garment and the wearer.

3 Elaborate decoration should not be used on poor materials.

4 On garments which will be frequently washed it is important that the decoration will also stand up to laundering.

5 The wrong side of the decoration should be as neat as the right side.

6 The decoration must in no way weaken the decorated portion of the garment.

EMBROIDERY STITCHES

These are usually used on undergarments where dainty effects may be obtained with a combination of simple stitches.

These stitches should only be used sparingly and with great skill on outer garments, as it is very easy to obtain a 'home-made', amateurish effect otherwise.

Only a few of the more simple embroidery stitches are shown here. Simple decoration in coloured stranded cottons or silk threads can be used to advantage on many garments but it is a mistake to spend much time in embroidery on inferior materials or on badly made garments.

Chain Stitch
This may be worked as a single or double-coloured chain and should give the appearance of even backstitch on the wrong side. It may be used as an outline or a filling stitch.

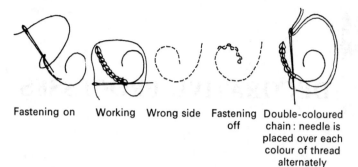

Fastening on   Working   Wrong side   Fastening off   Double-coloured chain: needle is placed over each colour of thread alternately

Stem Stitch

This stitch should also look like backstitch on the wrong side. The needle must be brought out at the same side of the preceding stitch each time. Used as an outline stitch.

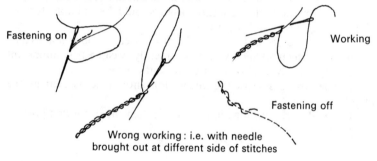

Fastening on   Working

                                                    Fastening off

Wrong working: i.e. with needle brought out at different side of stitches

Satin Stitch

Used for filling shapes. It may be worked with horizontal or sloping stitches, although it is often easier to make a finely-pointed shape with sloping ones.

rs   rs   ws

Fastening on   Working   Fastening off

Variations of Loopstitch and Herringbone

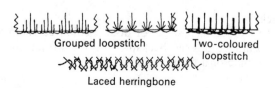

Grouped loopstitch   Two-coloured loopstitch

Laced herringbone

French Knots

Used for filling shapes, making centres to flowers, etc.

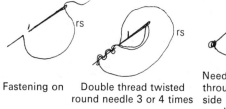

Fastening on   Double thread twisted   Needle taken
round needle 3 or 4 times   through to wrong
side after pulling
needle through
twisted threads

SHELL EDGING

This is a dainty, easily worked edge for fine materials and is equally suitable for frilled or straight edges. The size of each shell depends upon the texture of the material but, naturally, the smaller it is the daintier the effect. It is important that every shell should be the same size.

Working

    1 The edge is worked from the wrong side, the hem being turned in the fingers as the work progresses. As it must be a very narrow hem, tacking is not necessary.

    2 Fasten on with a firm, double stitch, slip the needle between the thicknesses of the hem, then work an oversewing stitch over the hem, pulling the thread tightly, to form the 'shell'. Bring the needle out to the right of the thread when working the oversewing stitch in order to 'lock' it.

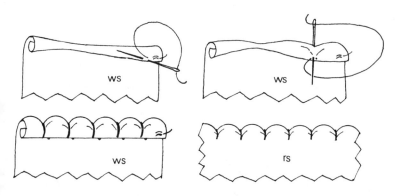

Note: Take care, when joining on a fresh thread, that the double stitches required for fastening on and off are worked at the bottom of one of the oversewing stitches. In this way there should be no break in the shells.

F

As well as using this as a method of fixing a hem it is possible to shell-edge the fold of tucks and bindings to give added decoration. This method is very suitable for blouse finishes.

Shell-edged tucks 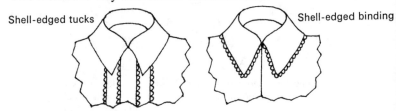 Shell-edged binding

PIN STITCH

This stitch is worked in a similar manner to the normal hem stitch used in drawn-thread work, but

    a it is usually a much smaller stitch

    b no threads are drawn out, the perforated effect being produced by the thickness of the needle and the pulling tight of the thread

    c it may be worked on curves and other shapes instead of only to a straight thread.

It may be used to secure hems, seams or appliquéd sections.

The stitch is worked on the right side, therefore, if the hem cannot be turned to this side, the stitch must be worked along the line of the hem as seen from the right side. Fasten on thread with a double stitch on the double material.

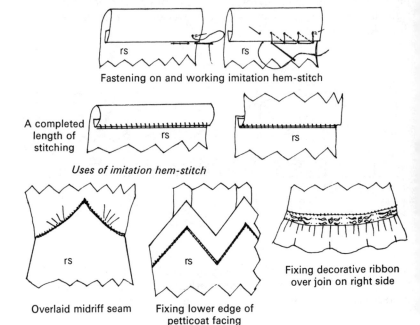

Fastening on and working imitation hem-stitch

A completed length of stitching

Uses of imitation hem-stitch

Overlaid midriff seam

Fixing lower edge of petticoat facing

Fixing decorative ribbon over join on right side

FACED SCALLOPING

This method makes a neat and attractive hemline for sleeve and neck edges of dresses and for the skirt hems of children's dresses. The principle is the same as for any shaped facing (see p. 59) but care must be taken to see that the scallops are even in shape and carefully stitched to avoid fraying of turned edges.

Method

    1 Make a pattern, or template, of the required size and shape of scallops, using coins or compasses and thin card.

Making the template

Draw a straight line on a piece of thin card and mark out the required size of the scallops by drawing circles of the same diameter.

    Draw a line through the circles at their points of contact with each other.

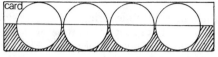

    Cut out the card between the lower curves.

    The number of scallops depends on the shape of the edge to be faced. On a straight edge any number may be used and repeated as often as necessary. On a curved edge one or two only should be used on the template.

    2 If a symmetrical effect is required it is advisable to measure the edge first and make the scallops of a diameter which is evenly divisible into the length of the edge (e.g. on a 22 cm edge, 4 scallops of 5·5 cm are preferable to 5½ 4 cm scallops).

    3 When a neck edge is to be scalloped the curves should be arranged from the centre front, evenly spaced outwards in both directions.

Sleeve edge with scallops

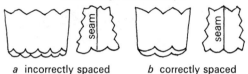

a incorrectly spaced   *b* correctly spaced

Neck edge with scallops

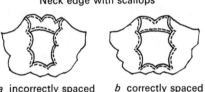

a incorrectly spaced   *b* correctly spaced

4 Draw round the outline of the scallops on the wrong side of the garment edge, the deepest part of the curve to the fitting line.

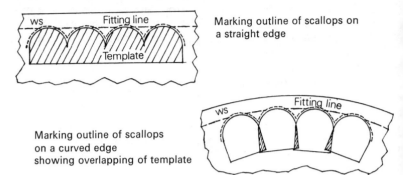

Marking outline of scallops on a straight edge

Marking outline of scallops on a curved edge showing overlapping of template

5 Place the right side of the facing to the right side of the garment and tack with small stitches along the outline of the scallops.

Tack facing and garment together as shown to prevent stitching from pulling the facing out of position.

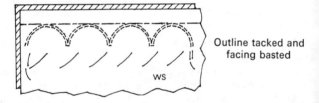

Outline tacked and facing basted

6 Stitch along shaped outline by machine or firmly by hand, making one stitch between the scallops parallel to the fitting line. Remove tackings. Cut turnings to shape, 6 mm deep.

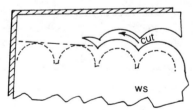

7 Clip diagonally round curves and straight into points between scallops.

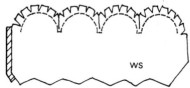

8 Turn facing to wrong side of garment, work out seam of scallops, removing all 'pockets'. Tack at edge to hold in position. Press lightly. Remove tackings and re-press; or edge-stitch, remove tackings and press.

If scallops are deep and facing is narrow, turn under edge of facing and neaten with small running stitches, leaving edge free.

Otherwise, neaten the free edge of the facing with machine edge-stitch and catch into position on seams.

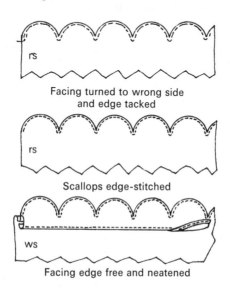

Facing turned to wrong side
and edge tacked

Scallops edge-stitched

Facing edge free and neatened

Note: On fully lined garments the lining may be used to neaten the scallops instead of an additional facing.

WORKED SCALLOPING

This is an attractive and dainty method of finishing the edges of lingerie and may be used on fine cottons as well as on most other fine lingerie fabrics.

Care should be taken not to make the scallops too large: the smaller the curves the daintier the effect. The shape of the scallops may be marked on the wrong side of the material by using scalloping transfer strips which may be purchased in many different sizes, arrangements and colours. Yellow is by far the most suitable colour on all but yellow fabric (see *Carbon Paper*, p. 115). Alternatively, a template in two different positions as described on the next page may be used.

Making the template
Make a row of circles against a straight line by drawing round a disc of the required size on a piece of thin card.

Draw a line through the points of contact and cut away the card between the curves (shaded portion of diagram).

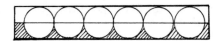

When preparing a template with shallow curves, overlap the circles at the same distance at the line of the diameter.

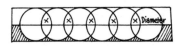

Curves produced by discs placed side by side

Curves produced by discs overlapping

Method
1 Draw round template on right side of fabric, using a chalk pencil or a white or yellow crayon (if a commercial iron-on transfer has been used, tack out the edge of the scallops through to the right side). Leave 1·3 cm turning between deepest part of curve and edge of garment.

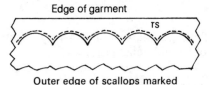

Outer edge of scallops marked

2 Mark inner edge of scallops by using same template with centre dropped for the required depth of scallop.

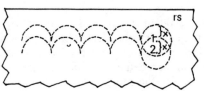

Inner edge of scallops marked

x = distance between centres of circles and depth of widest part of scallop

3 Work scallops with either loopstitch or buttonhole stitch, making the stitches close together and with the looped or knotted edge towards the outer edge of the garment. Keep stitches straight and work right up into each point.

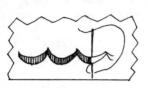

Scallops with loopstitch   Scallops with buttonhole stitch

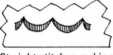

Straight stitches making
firm points

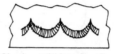

Sloping stitches forming
weak points

4 If extra firmness and a slightly raised effect are required, the scallops may first be padded with rows of running or chain stitch, before loopstitch is worked.

Padded with running stitches

Padded with chain stitches

5 Using very sharp, pointed scissors cut away the material outside the purl edge of the scallops, taking care not to cut the stitches.

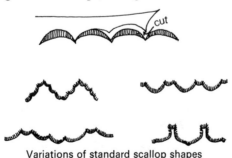

Variations of standard scallop shapes

APPLIQUÉ

This is a decorative method of applying one material to another. It is an effective decoration for children's wear, beachwear, slips and household articles. Very attractive effects may be obtained by using contrasting textures, e.g. seerloop on poplin, poplin on towelling, needlecord on denim.

Method

    1 Cut out the desired shape and apply to the right side of the garment.

    2 Tack motif in position on the right side of the garment and stitch into position. Work close machine zig-zag or satin stitch over raw edges.

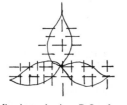

| Shape firmly tacked to R.S. of material, working from centre outwards | Shape stitched into position and neatened with zig-zag or satin stitch |

    3 Additional features may be added with embroidery stitches. Some details, e.g. leaf veins, may be embroidered before the shape is applied.

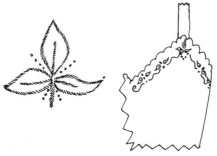

Appliquéd motifs with simple embroidery stitches

NET APPLIQUÉ (DÉCOUPÉ)

On fine fabrics a most attractive effect may be obtained by applying net or organdie to the wrong side of the material and afterwards cutting away the garment material from the right side, leaving the shape carried out in contrast fabric only.

Method

    1 Transfer the chosen shape to the garment material on the wrong side.

    2 Tack a double layer of the fine material over the shape on the wrong side of the garment.

    3 Outline the design in zig-zag or satin stitch, taking care to keep the stitches close together.

    4 Complete the motif with satin stitch where required.

    5 Cut away surplus contrast material from outside of motif and garment material from right side of motif.

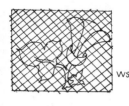 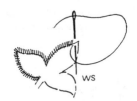 

APPLIQUÉ EDGES

A similar method may be used for making an attractive edging to lingerie by means of a double fold of material used in conjunction with scalloping or other satin-stitched edges.

Method

    1 Place a fold of net (chiffon, satin or patterned fabric) behind the edge of the garment and tack it into position.

    Work the edge with buttonhole stitch, zig-zag or satin stitch.

    2 Cut away surplus garment material from the right side of the garment and surplus trimming material from the back.

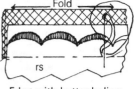

Edge with buttonholing

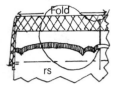

Edge with satin stitch

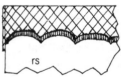

Surplus material cut away
from worked edge

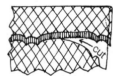

Surplus fine material cut away
from back of garment

SHADOW WORK

On thin and semi-transparent materials, motifs can be effectively worked by outlining the shape in tiny backstitches, the thread being taken across the back of the motif between each two stitches. In this way the design is outlined in the colour of the thread used. Very effective results may be obtained by using either contrasting or matching colours, white thread on white material being one successful method.

Method

    1 Draw or transfer the motif to the wrong side of the material, as faintly as possible.

    2 Work closed herringbone stitch across the design, making sure that stitches are even and leave no gaps in the outline. Use one strand of embroidery thread.

Motif worked on wrong side   Working stitching

    3 Complete motif on right side with necessary embroidery stitches.

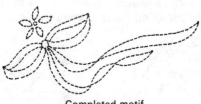

Completed motif

Note: Great care must be taken in fastening stitches on and off. To fasten on, make a knot in the thread, put the needle into the work from the right side, about 2 cm along the design, bringing it out at the starting point. Work the stitches over the thread lying along the wrong side of the design and cut the knot off afterwards. When fastening off, weave the end carefully into the crossed stitches as close to the outline as possible.

BRODERIE ANGLAISE

This is a French name for a typically English type of embroidery—the literal translation is 'English embroidery'. It is a simple form of embroidery and is most effective on fine cottons and other firmly woven lingerie materials, especially when worked in self-colour. A sharp, pointed pair of scissors and a stiletto are essential.

Method

1 Transfer or draw the design on to the wrong side of the material as lightly as possible.

2 Outline the edge of the design in small running stitches, without fastening on the thread. Do not cut thread.

3 Using sharp, pointed scissors, cut across the material within the outline in both directions. For round holes push stiletto through to required diameter.

4 Working from the right side, tuck the raw edges of the cut sections back and work close satin stitches over the outlined shape. Trim off excess material on the wrong side.

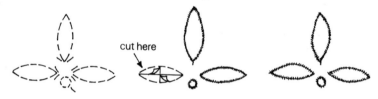

5 Complete design with other simple embroidery stitches such as stem stitch and French knots.

FAGGOTING

This stitch may be used as an insertion for joining together two panels (e.g. down the front of a blouse) or to make a dainty, attractive edging for lingerie with a rouleau tube. It can be used on most materials with equal effect.

Preparation of edge of garment or panel
Make as narrow a turning as possible on the right side. Secure the turning with running or machine-stitches. Turn edge in again to wrong side and tack.

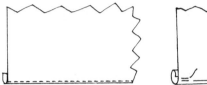 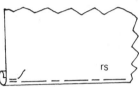

Preparation of edging strip
Prepare a rouleau from a crossway strip (see p. 40) or fold and tack a straight strip as shown.

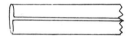 

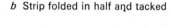

a Straight strip with turnings   *b* Strip folded in half and tacked
folded towards centre

Crossway rouleau

Note: If edge to be decorated is curved, a crossway rouleau of the required width should be used; if straight, a straight strip is satisfactory.
Method
    1 On to a strip of stout paper tack the edge of the garment and the edging strip at the required distance apart. (Draw lines on paper first to make sure that edges are parallel.)

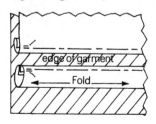

2 Fasten on thread at left-hand side with a tiny double stitch and continue by working one of the following:

a Criss-cross Faggoting

Take the thread diagonally across the space from the upper to the lower edge, placing the needle behind the previous stitch each time as shown.

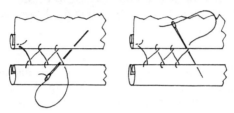

b Bar Faggoting

Fasten on as before and take the thread straight across the space to the opposite edge.

Twist the needle under and over the bar formed and pull it through.

Take needle through the upper edge, slip it through the hem to the position of the next stitch and repeat.

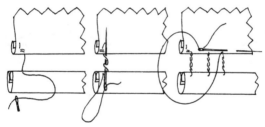

Note: To increase the decorative effect the rouleau may be shell-edged before it is attached to the garment with faggoting.

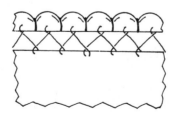

LACE

Lace must always be set on garments by hand and is usually stitched on the right side of the garment. The lace used should be as far as possible of a similar thread to the material on which it is used (e.g. cotton lace on cambric, nylon lace on nylon).

It should be of as good quality as can be afforded, the danger being that lace of poor quality often wears out before the garment and is also inclined to shrink.

EDGING LACE

1 The most easily worked method for very fine fabrics is to roll the edge of the material in the fingers and whip it, catching in the edge of the lace at the same time. The lace may be gathered by pulling up its straight thread if required.

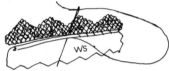

2 If preferred the lace may be attached by a narrow (bight 1½–2) machine satin stitch. Excess raw edges on the wrong side may be trimmed away close to the stitching.

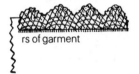

Edge of lace satin-stitched
to garment edge

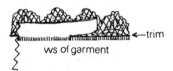

Surplus fabric trimmed away
from wrong side

LACE JOIN

1 Overlap lace so that patterns coincide.

2 Run or machine-stitch around design outline and satin stitch over.

3 Trim excess lace away close to stitching on right and wrong sides.

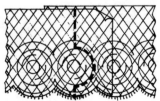

Lace pattern overlapped and two layers joined with running or straight machine-stitch

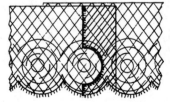

Satin stitch worked over join and overlapping lengths of lace trimmed away

DECORATIVE MACHINE-STITCHING

A very smart, tailored effect can be obtained simply by using rows of machine-stitching, especially on cuffs, collars and pocket edges. It is essential that rows of stitches are evenly spaced and perfectly straight. Corners must be sharp and stitches should not be allowed to 'cut' corners. The machine foot itself is a good guide for this stitching, each succeeding row being the width of either the small or the wide part of the foot away from the next. Interesting braid effects can be obtained by careful selection and matching of swing-needle stitches. A transparent foot is obtainable from several manufacturers of these machines which makes matching and positioning easier.

This is a method of decoration which is not recommended until the worker is very much in command of the machine.

Variations of effect may be produced by using a thick thread on the bobbin and a matching thinner one on the reel, and by various arrangements of rows.

Besides being decorative this method produces a slight stiffening in the material and prevents crumpling, particularly of collars.

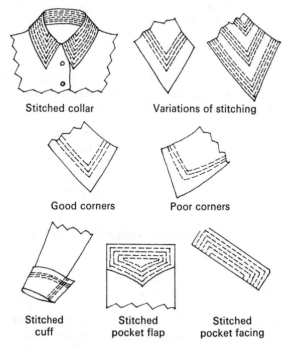

Stitched collar   Variations of stitching

Good corners   Poor corners

Stitched cuff   Stitched pocket flap   Stitched pocket facing

SMOCKING

Smocking is a form of gathering in which several rows are worked and embroidered. The name comes from the gathered smocks or overalls worn by country folk in bygone days. These were made of very strong, hard-wearing cotton material which lasted for years. In fact, hand-embroidered smocks were often heirlooms, and they have now become a traditional form of English handiwork.

Nowadays smocking is worked on a large variety of materials—cottons, silks, nylons, rayons and even velvets. Although most often used on children's garments it also forms a delightful method of shaping and decorating blouses and nightdresses for adults.

The amount of material required varies slightly according to the stitches used for the surface embroidery and also according to the tension at which individuals work. Generally, three times the finished width is a satisfactory proportion. When completed the smocked portions should be quite elastic and should regain their original width automatically after being stretched out.

The basic stitches used in smocking are comparatively few and simple, the variety of design depending on the arrangement of these stitches and the colour schemes chosen.

Preparation of Material

There are three ways in which material may be prepared for the gathering necessary for the embroidery.

The stitches must be worked over even folds rather like miniature organ pipes in appearance, and to gain this effect it is essential that the gathers are worked exactly in line with each other, thus:

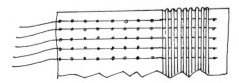

To obtain these even rows of stitches one of these methods should be used:

1 Material may be marked out with pencil dots, using a ruler for exact measurements. This is, however, a somewhat laborious method for any but the smallest width of smocking and may leave obstinate marks.

2 Use a smocking transfer. Transfers may be bought in various sizes—the smaller the spaces between the dots the finer the finished effect. In order that no transfer ink is visible on the right side it is advisable to place the transfer face downwards upon the wrong side of the material before pressing with a warm iron.

Picking up spots made from smocking transfers

3 It is sometimes possible to use the weave or design of the material to gauge the gathers. For example, excellent effects may be obtained by picking up alternate squares of finely checked gingham. In this way it is possible to produce quite distinctive results by using either the right or wrong side (e.g. on red/white checked gingham, where the white checks are picked up, an all-over white effect is obtained on one side and a red effect on the other).

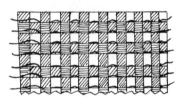

Using checks to gauge position of gathers

Spotted materials may also be used in this way, but it must be borne in mind that printed spots rarely lie on the straight of the material. To obtain the best results it is advisable for the gathers to be worked on a straight thread, preferably the weft, so that the warp threads lie down the gathers.

Working Gathering

1 This is one of the very few occasions on which it is advisable to start with a knot. In this way the end of the thread may easily be grasped and pulled back when the embroidery has been completed.

2 Make sure that each thread is long enough to work the complete width of gathering without joining.

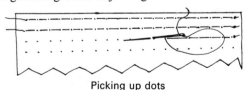

Picking up dots

3 When the required number of rows have been worked, cut off all ends to the same length, pull up each pair of rows separately and wind the threads round a pin at the required tension (i.e. with the gathered portion the same width as the fitted portion to which it is to be joined). Alternatively, fit to a template cut to the same shape as required for the finished garment. (Use this method if the smocked section is not fitted to a yoke, cuff, band, etc.)

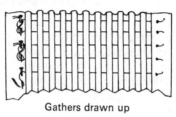

Gathers drawn up

Finished Smocking

The smocked portion may be set on to a yoke, cuff or band in the normal manner.

If the smocked section itself forms the yoke or band (e.g. round-necked smock or nightdress, wrist finish for a shirt sleeve), a very narrow rolled or whipped hem should be worked before the foundation gathers are put in. The gathers should be drawn up to fit a shaped template and the first row of smocking should be a line of outline stitch at a firm tension to prevent the finished work from stretching.

BASIC SMOCKING STITCHES

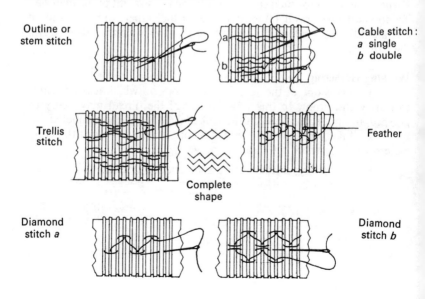

Outline or stem stitch

Cable stitch:
a single
b double

Trellis stitch

Complete shape

Feather

Diamond stitch a

Diamond stitch b

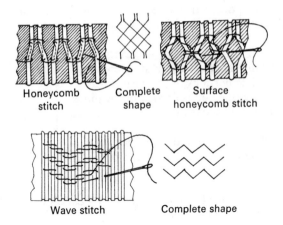

Honeycomb stitch   Complete shape   Surface honeycomb stitch

Wave stitch   Complete shape

FURTHER STUDY

THINGS TO DO

1 Make suitable designs for appliqué, broderie anglaise and shadow work motifs.

2 Make specimens of the processes described in the preceding chapter. Prepare a folder for each process and include details of its use.

3 Collect illustrations of decorative processes for reference.

4 Find as many different types of embroidery thread as possible. Find out their prices and the nature of the fibres.

QUESTIONS TO ANSWER

1 Complete the following statements by filling in the blank spaces with words taken from the right-hand column:

a .... is an embroidery stitch worked like backstitch (w.s.) on the right side of the fabric and used to outline shapes or form 'stems' on small floral motifs.	machine stitch
	herringbone
b Worked scallops may be made with either buttonhole stitch or	embroidery
c Shadow work is formed with closely packed .... stitches.	faggoting
d A useful filling for the centres of embroidered flowers or to give a 'seeded' appearance is spaced	découpé
	loopstitch
e 'Flower petals' and small solid shapes are best worked in	appliqué
f Two sections of fabric or a garment edge and a rouleau may be decoratively joined together by	stem stitch

g A smart decorative effect for tailored collars and cuffs may be achieved by working parallel rows of ....

h .... is a method of decorating garments by stitching shapes of contrasting colour or fabric onto suitable portions of the garments.

i When this method is carried out with net and the garment fabric cut away to reveal it the method is called ....

j Smocking is a method of decorating garments by working rows of .... over panels of gathered fabric.

French knots

satin stitch

2 Give details for finishing the hem of a child's dress with faced scallops. The hem would be approximately 9 cm.

3*a* Sketch a design for embroidery to be used on the bib front of shorts *or* trousers. Name a suitable type of fabric for the shorts *or* trousers and indicate the colour you would choose.

b Give clearly-labelled diagrams and brief notes for working the embroidery.

c Name the type(s) of thread(s) and colour(s) you would use to work the embroidery. (C.U.B.)

4*a* Show by sketches how the introduction of smocking can be an attractive feature on a dress for yourself.

Name a suitable type of fabric for the dress and indicate the colour you would choose.

b Give clearly-labelled diagrams and brief notes on:

(*i*) preparing for the smocking

(*ii*) working two smocking stitches to be used.

c Name the type and colour(s) of the thread(s) you would use for working the smocking on the dress. (C.U.B.)

5 Suggest *two* types of decoration which are in fashion at the moment.

List the order of work for *one* type. (C. & G.)

6 Suggest a type of decoration suitable for *each* of the following:

a a christening robe in fine lawn

b a little girl's dress in Viyella

c a black nylon blouse.

Describe, with sketches, how to work *one* type of decoration.

(C. & G.)

5

CHILDREN'S GARMENTS

The days in which children's clothes were merely smaller versions of those their parents wore are long past and nowadays children are considered deserving of fashions of their own. To buy all their clothes ready-made is an expensive business, however, and much money can be saved by home-dressmaking.

Nearly gone, too, is the day of intricate hand-work, especially on babies' clothes. In modern small families there is far less 'handing down' of·garments and they are therefore not usually made for long-term use. Some simple decoration is always in order, though, and charming effects may be obtained by very quickly worked methods.

CHOOSING CHILDREN'S CLOTHES

Children grow too fast to make it a practical proposition to allow for two separate sets of garments, one of which is to be worn only occasionally. Even so, it is obviously common sense to provide clothes which don't matter for playing in and better ones for more formal occasions.

As there will certainly always be some large portion of the wardrobe in the wash, the number of garments required is usually more than is necessary in later years. This is yet another reason for practising economy.

Children should be taught to take care of their clothes as early as possible. As they are trained to dress themselves they may also be encouraged to hang up and fold the garments they take off.

MATERIALS

1 *Materials chosen must be easily laundered.* This is an important point to be considered through the years until well into adolescence, when young people can reasonably be expected to take care of their own clothes.

Cottons of all weights (up to that of denim) and most finishes are ideal for children's garments, as they are comfortable to wear and easily washed and ironed. Synthetic fabrics are popular for babies' and young children's wear, but these should be used with great care as much woven synthetic fabric is not very absorbent. They are, however, extremely easy to wash and dry and to iron when necessary. Mixtures of wool and cotton such as Viyella and Clydella, and woollen fabrics with shrink-resist and machine-washable finishes are especially suitable for children's winter wear. Hand-knitted woollen jerseys or cardigans may be added for extra warmth.

2 *Materials chosen should be hard-wearing.* Thick materials are not necessarily those which will last longest. If loosely woven, even the bulkiest fabrics will pull out of shape with continuous wear and the threads will show signs of parting at seams. Finer, closely-woven fabrics will often stand up to considerably greater strain.

3 *Materials should be as non-inflammable as possible.* Almost all fabrics, particularly those with fluffy or napped surfaces, are inflammable and great care must be taken when children are likely to be close to an unguarded fire, as when undressing and at parties. Cotton fabrics may be treated to render them less dangerous.

Only wool and the modacrylic fibre Teklan are not inflammable and will smoulder too slowly to present any danger. (See p. 211.)

Nylon is very inflammable, forming a sticky bead which quickly hardens and will cause nasty burns on the skin. (See p. 229.)

The safest course is to treat all materials as inflammable and to protect children by using fire-guards over any type of fire, thus avoiding the slightest risk.

4 *Colour and pattern should be suitable for the wearer.* Colours should be chosen to suit the colouring of the child and preference given as soon as possible to his or her own choice. Patterns, however attractive, should not be too large, as they are then out of proportion to the size of the garment.

Colours should not be chosen because they 'don't show the dirt'. The dirt will be there whatever the colour and it must be remembered that the non-absorbent synthetic fibres tend to lose anti-static finishes after repeated washings and therefore attract dirt more easily. These finishes can be partially renewed by the use of commercial fabric softeners and rinses during laundering. Smooth-surfaced and glazed fabrics are more resistant to dirt than fluffy or textured ones and many materials, especially cottons, can be bought with stain-resistant or water-repellent finishes.

5 *The material should not be too expensive.* Few families, unless there are several children fairly close in age, can afford to lay aside little-worn garments. Nevertheless, fabrics of as good quality as can be reasonably afforded will be easier to handle in the making up and present a better finished appearance than cheap ones.

STYLES

1 *The style chosen should be one which is easily laundered.* All

children's garments require frequent washing and should therefore not rely on elaborate shaping or decoration for their attraction, if the fabrics chosen are not easily drip-dried. Ruched panels are extremely difficult to iron satisfactorily, while button-through styles are particularly convenient, especially in shirts and blouses. Garments of this type, while equally easy to iron, often present the disadvantage of torn buttonholes and pulled-away buttons.

2 *The style of the garment must allow for it to be easily put on and off.* This entails long openings from the neck, loose sleeve-bands, no closely-fitted seams, easily managed fastenings. (Ribbons are preferable to buttons and buttonholes for very young children; Velcro touch-and-close fasteners are very satisfactory for toddler's clothes, particularly when they are learning to dress themselves.)

3 *It must allow for the growth of the child.* The garment should not be made to fit a child perfectly at present unless there is some way in which it can be lengthened later. Between the ages of one and ten children wear garments whose general shape gradually becomes less square and more oblong. After ten, figures begin to take shape as waists become defined in girls and shoulders broaden in boys. After this time length and breadth increase fairly rapidly.

4 *The style should not involve elaborate decoration.* Smocking, appliqué and machine embroidery are popular methods of decoration for children's clothes and are equally suitable for both boys' and girls' garments.

Gathers, frills, tucks and pleats may also be used to advantage, although small pleats should be avoided if the fabric is not composed of 55% or more synthetic fibre or is not treated with a permanent press finish, as they require careful and frequent pressing to look well.

Coloured braids, bindings and ribbons may also be used to make simple but effective decorative bands on skirts, sleeves and bodices. There are now delightful ribbons specially woven for children with animal or figure motifs. These wash well and, being quite substantial, may often be removed from worn-out garments and used again on new ones.

5 *Sleeves should be of a reasonable size and should not be tight-fitting.* If they are very small, puffed sleeves are difficult to iron and to put on a small child. Therefore drip-dry materials should be chosen and, for toddlers unable to dress themselves, the sleeve-band should be big enough to admit adult fingers.

Making Provision for Growth

Ready-made garments for children can now be purchased with double seams and hems which may be let out and down as the child grows. Provision of this kind is especially valuable in teenagers' school uniforms and other expensive outfits.

With a little thought the home dressmaker too can make children's clothes which, while fitting well at the time they are made, may be easily and satisfactorily enlarged later.

MAKING UP GARMENTS

1 Choose style carefully—i.e. raglan sleeves rather than set-in, semi-fitting rather than tight-fitting dresses (especially at the waist), separates rather than one-piece garments—to ensure that a child's garment has a longer life.

2 Use a pattern a little larger than the actual size required and make deep turnings on all seams.

Use flat (or open) seams rather than French ones. A flat seam with wide turnings is less bulky than a French one of the same width and is much easier to let out.

3 Make deep turnings at waist and shoulder joins, to allow the skirt to be dropped from the waist and the bodice from the shoulders.

Yokes are convenient places for letting down, the gathered portions fitted into them providing ample extra width for the growing body. Any alteration made from the shoulders will, however, affect the sleeve and collar fittings. Sleeves which are slightly gathered in the first place may be let out as the armhole size is increased; but collars are not easily altered and, rather than having a badly fitted one, the enlarged neckline should be finished with either a binding or a new collar.

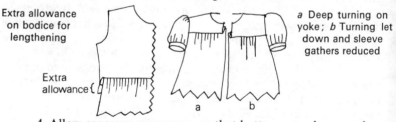

Extra allowance on bodice for lengthening

Extra allowance {

a Deep turning on yoke; *b* Turning let down and sleeve gathers reduced

a   b

4 Allow generous wrapovers, so that buttons may be moved as increasing width is required.

5 On skirts, shorts and crawlers which are supported by straps, work the buttonholes on the waistband and move the button down the strap as necessary.

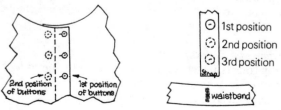

⊖ 1st position
⊙ 2nd position
⊝ 3rd position

Strap

waistband

2nd position of buttons   1st position of buttons

Buttons may be moved to increase width and length

6 Make deep hems on sleeves, lower edges of blouses and shirts, trouser legs, bottoms of skirts, etc.

These should always be worked by hand, not only because hand-finishing is neater than machine-finishing but also because it is easier to remove.

7 Add tucks to bodices and skirts to provide present decoration and allowance for future lengthening and widening.

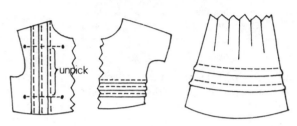

8 Shrink material before it is cut out if there is the slightest risk of shrinkage during washing. To do this, press the entire length with a hot iron over damp muslin. A great deal of trouble and disappointment will be saved by buying fabrics with a shrink-resist finish.

ALTERING OUT-GROWN GARMENTS

1 Let out tucks.
2 Let down hems.
3 Let out seams.

Note: All these alterations should be made before washing the garment, so that stitch-holes will close in laundering.

4 Lengthen skirts.

a Undo existing hem completely and face it.

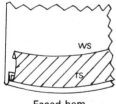

Faced hem

A plain material of similar colour may be used for the false hem or commercial hem-facing may be purchased. On a curved hem the facing should be cut to the same shape with seams corresponding to those in the skirt, or cut on the cross and eased or stretched as shown on p. 54. On straight hems the facing may be a straight strip.

or b Cut through the skirt in two or more places and insert strips of contrasting material or ribbon. Seams in the insertion must correspond with those in the skirt.

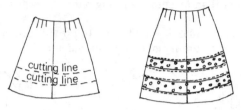

The contrasting bands should be inserted by means of overlaid seams and a little of the same fabric used somewhere on the bodice as a trimming in order to make the alteration less discernible (e.g. as binding to collar and sleeves; bow at neck; covering material for buttons, etc.).

5 Lengthen bodices.

Insert shaped waistband at back and front. This may be cut from material which contrasts in colour or pattern with that of the garment (e.g. a plain colour used on figured material, figured on plain, etc.).

This method of lengthening is particularly suitable for dresses for young teenagers, where waist shaping is beginning to be necessary.

6 Widen bodices.

It is often necessary to provide extra width on the front of teenagers' dresses while the rest of the garment is still of a suitable size. In these cases an attractive method is to cut down the bodice front to the waist and insert a 'dickey' of a plain material; white makes an effective contrast and if this is used the dickey should be detachable for frequent washing.

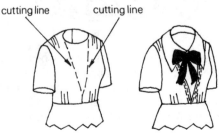

7 Alter tight sleeves.

Cut down too-short long sleeves to above elbow and re-hem them.

Or shape lower edge of a straight sleeve and re-face.

Or puff sleeves which have become too small may be cut and have their edges neatened, forming frilled sleeves.

cutting line

8 Alter tight necks.

Remove collar, cut down neck to required size and bind.

Or reshape neck entirely and face raw edges.

To cut the new neckline, pin shoulder seams together and also centre front and back of bodice. Cut to required shape through double material.

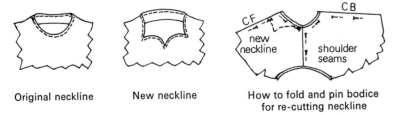

Original neckline   New neckline   How to fold and pin bodice for re-cutting neckline

9 Make a skirt from a dress which is altogether too tight.

Remove the bodice from the skirt and cut straight strips from it 5–7·5 cm wide. Use these to make a waistband on which to mount the skirt, and for ornamental straps if required. Use crossway strips of the bodice material to bind the neck and armholes of a plain blouse so that it matches the skirt.

CHILDREN'S GARMENTS FROM ADULTS'

Many adults' garments are laid aside long before they are worn out, either because they are no longer in fashion or because they require more alteration to make them fit than the wearer can cope with. Much of the material in these garments is still good and an imaginative needlewoman may save a fair amount of money by converting them into garments for children.

Rules for adapting garments

    1 Aim at a finished result which does not look like a 'make-do'

effort. Use only materials, colours and patterns which would be chosen if new fabric were being purchased.

2 Take the original garment to pieces completely, saving any buttons or other fastenings which may be used again. Wash and press the pieces and cut away all badly worn or faded portions.

3 Make sure of the direction of the selvedge threads in each piece and place the paper pattern in position as you would in new material.

Suggestions for adaptations of garments

Matinée jackets or dresses cut from skirt portion of adult's nightdress (this usually wears at the top long before the lower part is worn).

Girl's summer dress cut down to pinafore dress for younger child (avoiding use of worn underarm sections).

Small boy's shorts cut from lower portion of flannel skirt (avoiding 'seated' area).

Boy's shorts cut from a plain cotton gaberdine skirt too tight for the previous owner.

Child's coat cut from blanket-cloth dressing-gown turned and dyed.

Child's dress cut from discarded crêpe blouse (decoration on blouse may often be incorporated into small dress, either on yoke or scattered on skirt).

Small pyjamas cut from large ones worn at shoulders and crutch.

FURTHER STUDY

THINGS TO DO

1 Collect pictures or make drawings of a complete outfit for a child (specify age; and include underwear, outerwear and beach wear). Add specimens of suitable fabrics to each illustration and compare prices of similar garments *a.* bought ready-made and *b.* made at home.

2 Make a child's garment, choosing a style which makes the best allowance for growth. Incorporate a decorative finish which will attract the child.

3 Make a study of children's garments through the ages, using portraits, museums, photographs and literature as sources of information.

QUESTIONS TO ANSWER

1 Complete the following statements by filling in the blanks with words taken from the right-hand column:

a Children's nightwear is often made from brushed cotton fabric and care must be taken to choose that which has been treated to make it .... | drip-dry

pinafore dress

b Wool is a truly flame-resistant fabric; .... is also a flame-resistant fabric suitable for children's wear.

c When making children's dresses and jackets .... must be made large enough for comfort and for adults' hands to be able to help them on.

d The best type of sleeve for children to get into and to remain comfortable as they grow is the .... style.

e An easy-to-use fastening for small fingers which cannot manage buttons or hooks is ....

f Viyella is a particularly good fabric for children's dresses and other garments because it is warm to wear, being partly wool, and is .... as well.

g Puffed sleeves in young children's dresses are attractive to look at but are difficult to iron and should, therefore, be made only in .... fabrics.

h When a new dress is being made for a little girl, ... in the bodice will allow for it to be let down as she grows.

i The easiest and quickest way of lengthening a skirt is to let down the ....; ample allowance should therefore be made when originally cutting the skirt.

j A child's dress which has become too tight under the arms and round the chest can be conveniently adapted into a ....

Velcro

hem

flame-resistant

Teklan

armholes

shrink-resistant

raglan

tucks

2 Suggest a complete outfit (day and night wear) for a four-year-old girl, illustrating your answers with sketches. Say what materials you would choose for the garment and give your reasons.

3*a* Sketch outfits suitable for four-year-old twins (a boy and a girl) to wear to a party.

b What fabrics would you choose? Give your reasons.

c Make a shopping list of all the items you would need for making these outfits.   (A.E.B.)

4*a* Suggest, with the help of sketches, *three* different ways of lengthening a young girl's cotton dress.

b Describe and illustrate the working of one of the methods you have sketched.   (A.E.B.)

6

UNDERWEAR

There is such a great variety of delightful ready-made underwear on sale at a reasonable price today that one is tempted to think that it is not worth making one's own. It must be remembered, however, that as the garments available are almost invariably made of nylon or Tricel knit and produced on a very tight budget control there is not much scope for the out-of-the-ordinary unless one is prepared to spend quite a considerable amount of money. For instance, it is often a near impossibility to find light cotton underwear or nightwear for a hot spell or for a summer holiday in the Mediterranean or tropical climates. There is also much satisfaction in producing pretty underwear oneself.

CHOICE OF MATERIAL

1 *Material suitable for underwear is absorbent.* If the moisture given off by the body is not absorbed, the skin is chilled and the wearer very uncomfortable. Cottons, woollen mixtures, silks and rayons are all satisfactory in this respect. Nowadays, however, synthetics are extensively used, which some people find more comfortable to wear than do others. Silk for underwear is difficult to come by. It is sometimes possible to buy silk *habutai* that is heavier than jap silk and produced for dyeing and printing. Sometimes special purchases, particularly of natural coloured silks, are available at prices comparable with top quality Swiss cotton in the larger department store chains.

Generally, a cellular or knitted construction is preferable to the plain woven fabric because air is more easily circulated. On the other hand, lack of absorption means quick drying, which is an asset in laundering.

2 *Material should be easily laundered.* Cleanliness is absolutely essential where underwear is concerned, as any accumulation of waste products from the body is bound to cause underwear to feel and smell unpleasant. Ease of washing and drying is therefore desirable, and modern manufacturers are making progress in producing fabrics which shed moisture quickly.

Many up-to-date materials also need little or no ironing (although even those labelled non-iron are often improved by light pressing). Mini-iron cottons, crease-resisting rayons and most synthetics are very satisfactory for petticoats and nightdresses, while some of the finer napped cotton/rayon fabrics and brushed nylons give extra warmth for winter nightwear without adding very much to the labour of laundering.

3 *It should not be bulky.* Most girls are so conscious of any element which prevents their outer garments from fitting well that it is hardly necessary to insist that fabrics chosen should be as fine as possible without detracting from the warmth required.

4 *It should be non-clinging.* Outer garments should slide easily over underwear in order to hang well and to be comfortable. Soft, rather slippery fabrics are therefore preferable to those with crêpe or fluffy surfaces (e.g. winceyette and Clydella are suitable for nightwear but not for petticoats). It should also be remembered that after repeated washings many synthetics lose their anti-static finish, attracting dirt and clinging to other fibres.

5 *Buy as good a quality as possible.* Cheap materials will not satisfactorily survive constant wear and washing for long and will soon show signs of pulling away at seams and across shoulders, seat and waist. At least three sets of underwear are advisable (the traditional 'one off, one on, and one in the wash') and these are expensive to replace frequently.

6 *Material should be attractive.* Most girls take so much pleasure and delight in their underwear that the choice of attractive materials is almost instinctive. It is well to remember, however, that the prettiest materials are not always the ones which will give best service, and quality as well as prettiness must be considered.

COLOUR

The colour of materials chosen is largely a matter of personal taste, but there are other considerations:

1 The colour of underwear should blend to some extent with that of the most generally worn outer garments (coloured slips often spoil the effect of fine white blouses).

2 Underwear should not be chosen because 'it doesn't show the dirt'. A dark slip worn under dark woollen skirts or dresses is quite sensible, because these do sometimes tend to discolour more delicate hues by rubbing on them; but it is essential to remember that a dark petticoat is as likely to become soiled as a white one and must be laundered as often.

STYLE

Again, personal taste is a large factor in choosing styles, but other considerations which must be taken into account are:

1 The undergarment should fit well beneath the outer garment, not only for the comfort of the wearer but also to allow the outer one to hang and fit satisfactorily.

2 The style of the underwear must correspond to that of the garments worn over it. Tailored suits, slim skirts and other casual garments require fitted, tailored underwear, while party dresses, long skirts and frilly blouses call for feminine underwear.

DECORATION

Attractive decoration provides a good deal of the appeal of underwear and is most enjoyable to carry out by hand. Care must be taken that:

1 Decoration is only applied to well-made garments. It is not suitable, for example, to apply expensive lace to a garment made with un-neatened seams, or to machine it to the raw edges of the garment. (See p. 166 for methods of applying lace.)

2 Any commercial trimming (lace, frilling, embroidered ribbon, etc.) must be of the same quality and as nearly as possible of the same nature as that of the garment, e.g. nylon should be trimmed with nylon lace and ribbon. This is necessary in order that the garment and the trimming wear and launder at the same rate.

3 The decoration should not be of too different a colour from that of the garment. It is unfortunate when the outline of brightly coloured embroidery is seen through a plain blouse, however attractive the embroidery is in itself.

Suitable decorative finishes (See pp. 151–66 for methods.) Appliqué, net work, shadow work, faggoting, shell-edging, broderie anglaise, lace, ribbon, embroidered motifs in simple line and filling stitches.

SEAMS

Seams chosen for underwear should be as dainty as possible while serving their purpose satisfactorily:

1 On petticoats and waist-slips French seams are most suitable as these are neat and dainty in appearance, prevent raw edges from fraying and show no stitching on the right side.

2 On pyjamas and nightdresses made from thicker materials double-stitched seams should be used. These are less bulky seams than French ones, they lie flat against the garment and they are not disarranged by ironing.

3 Petticoat or nightdress frills which are made from straight widths of material may be joined with flat or open seams. The selvedges of the material ensure that they will not fray and they are less bulky and easier to gather than French seams.

HEMS ON NIGHTDRESSES AND PETTICOATS

Hems of lingerie should be decorative as well as neatening the raw edges. They may be put up with a decorative stitch, e.g. satin stitch, and must be very narrow or double in the case of transparent fabrics.

Suitable methods for fine materials   (See pp. 151–66.) Rolled (with or without lace), shell-edged, finished with lace or net, scalloped (faced or worked), faggoted, frilled, imitation hem-stitched, bound.

Applying Frills
Cutting
Frills should always be cut with the selvedge threads running downwards, when the gathering or pleating sets very much better than if the selvedge threads run across.

Gathering
Frills should be gathered with two rows of stitching worked by hand or by machine. Alternatively, they may be pleated with the ruffler attachment supplied with most sewing machines. This forms a very attractive finish, is quickly worked and only one line of stitching is required. The attachment may be adjusted so that it pleats the strip at every few stitches or on every stitch. For most frills every fifth or sixth stitch gives a sufficiently full finish for which just under one and a half times the completed length of material is required. A finely pleated, very full frill can be obtained by pleating on every stitch and in this case three times the finished length is necessary. Finer adjustments may be made by making the stitch longer, thus making the spaces wider between the pleats.

This attachment fits over the screw holding the needle in position and can easily become loosened by the vibration of the ruffler. While working the frilling, therefore, check the needle screw frequently and tighten it if necessary. Practise on an odd piece of material before stitching the garment.

Attaching
Use an overlaid seam with the raw edges neatened with zig-zag or loop-stitching; or attach with 1·3 cm plain seam, trim frill to 6 mm and neaten with a self hem (see diagram); or machine frill to lower edge of garment on right side and cover raw edges with decorative ribbon held in position with straight or decorative machine stitching.

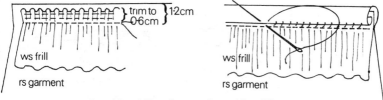

Attaching frill and neatening with self hem

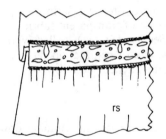

Ribbon covering raw edges and fixed
with decorative stitching

Decorative ribbon-carrier, sometimes known as *trou-trou* (lace) or beading, may be applied in the same way and narrow ribbon threaded through it.

On curved hems the upper edge of a straight trimming must be pleated or gathered at intervals to fit the curve. The lower edge should be fixed first so that sufficient length is used.

Attaching Shoulder Straps

Attach ribbons as for tapes. (See p. 32.) On points of petticoat tops the turning of the ribbon should be cut to shape. Stitches must be very tiny but quite secure.

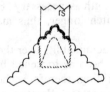

Inserting Elastic

1 Leave a space of about 2·5 cm in the second line of stitching on the casing or hem.

2 Pin one end of elastic to hem near the gap in the stitching and thread elastic through hem, making sure that it is not twisted. Use an elastic-threader or safety-pin.

3 Overlap the ends of the elastic and oversew them together along the edges. Hem the raw ends to the elastic.

4 Stitch the space left for threading.

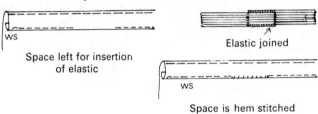

Space left for insertion
of elastic

Elastic joined

Space is hem stitched
(hand stitching eases access
for renewal of elastic)

Fastenings

Fastenings on all undergarments but pyjamas and nightdresses must be as inconspicuous as possible while still being efficient. They must be washable and not easily damaged by wringing or ironing.

1 Small buttons and buttonholes are suitable on waistbands, nightdresses and pyjamas. Velcro is a suitable alternative, especially on children's clothes.

2 The lightest weight zips, including nylon ones, should always be used on lingerie.

FURTHER STUDY

THINGS TO DO

1 Cost exactly a slip you could make for yourself from nylon jersey and compare *a.* the price and *b.* any apparent advantages with similar ready-made garments.

2 Make a study of underwear from 1900.

QUESTIONS TO ANSWER

1 Giving reasons for your choice, suggest two suitable materials for each of the following:

a children's nightwear

b lingerie for your own wear.

Show by labelled diagrams how to work:

c a seam for winter pyjamas

d a seam for a summer nightgown.

2 Describe, with the aid of diagrams and brief notes, the methods you would use to join the following:

a crossway strips

b the side seams of a rayon-crêpe nightgown

c a frill to the bottom of a petticoat.

In each case state the width of the seam.

3 Sketch a nightdress which you would like to make for yourself. Give details, illustrated with diagrams wherever possible, of the following:

a the fabric chosen

b the colour of the fabric and any haberdashery used

c the seams used

d the finish for the bottom hem.

4 With the aid of diagrams, explain exactly how to carry out the following processes:

a attaching a ribbon shoulder-strap to a petticoat

b attaching a frill to the bottom edge of a full-length waist slip

c applying lace to the wrist finish of a long-sleeved bed-jacket.

7

CARE OF CLOTHES

Girls of today are very conscious of the importance of good grooming and expend much time and interest on the care of their hair, hands and general appearance. The necessity for regular and careful attention to their clothes, new or well-worn, must be appreciated also, and it is never too early for girls to begin to take care of their own wardrobes.

EVERYDAY CARE OF CLOTHES

General rules

1 Never put away dirty garments.

2 Remove spots as soon as possible after they occur.

3 Brush outer garments before putting them away, and mend them if necessary.

4 Press clothes regularly.

5 Wash or dry-clean regularly.

6 Use hangers whenever possible. Thin dresses and blouses should be hung on padded hangers rather than plain wooden ones, and the hanger must be wide enough to support the shoulders of the garment without being too wide and causing peaks in sleeves.

7 Protect shoulders of hanging garments from dust with plastic or cotton covers, particularly those which are very light-coloured and which are worn only occasionally.

8 Remove brooches and other ornaments before putting away clothes, and take off detachable collars and cuffs immediately they look soiled.

9 Do not allow perfume or deodorant to come into contact with garments as it will become stale. Also, some thin fabrics are rotted by direct application of perfume or deodorants and some perfumes leave an ineradicable stain on fabrics.

UNDERWEAR

1 Never put away underwear which is soiled or which requires mending.

2 Store underwear—sorted into piles—in clean, lined drawers. Plastic, print, net, rayon or nylon sachets help to keep drawers tidy and attractive, and unwrapped tablets of perfumed soap, or bath cubes, placed among the garments, give underwear a clean, pleasant smell.

3 If it can be afforded, one complete set of underwear should always be kept ready and in good repair in case of unexpected journeys or other emergencies.

JUMPERS

1 Air well before putting away after washing and never store soiled woollen garments.

2 Do not wear until neckbands, elbows, and wrists become very dirty, as they will then require fairly hard rubbing which will damage the fibres.

3 Store woollens folded neatly in plastic bags to protect them from dust and from picking up dark fluff from other garments.

Note: Many girls wear tailored blouses under plain jumpers and this, besides having an attractive appearance, does help to prevent the wool from becoming quickly soiled.

SKIRTS

1 Brush, press and clean skirts regularly.

2 Store by hanging by loops from the waistband; or clipped into a skirt hanger; or folded carefully and hung over the rail of a hanger; or folded carefully lengthwise and laid flat in a drawer.

DRESSES

1 Hang up dresses immediately they are taken off, and air well before putting away. Place the buckle of the belt over the hook of the hanger so that it is ready to hand next time the dress is worn.

2 Use narrow tapes in the shoulders of sleeveless dresses to prevent shoulder straps from slipping. One end of the tape should be hemmed to the shoulder seam just under half-way along it; at the other end one half of a press-fastener should be sewn, the corresponding half being attached to the shoulder seam. Lingerie ribbon may be used instead of tape if preferred.

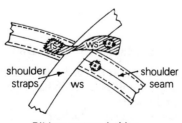

Ribbon or tape holder
for shoulder strap

STORING SUMMER CLOTHES

1 Wash all washable garments and have others dry-cleaned. Do not starch clothes. Pull them into shape, do any necessary repairs and fold them away in cases or drawers.

2 Place shoes on shoe-trees or pad them well with crumpled paper. Clean thoroughly and wrap in paper before storing.

3 Light woollen garments must be thoroughly dry before being put away, to prevent discoloration. If they are not guaranteed moth-proof, add one of the pleasanter moth deterrents and wrap them in tissue paper or plastic containers.

Avoid any danger of mildew, caused by storing damp garments, by making quite sure that all clothes are thoroughly dry and aired before storing.

STORING WINTER CLOTHES

1 Have garments commercially dry-cleaned if necessary.

2 Remove stains and spots from any garments not to be dry-cleaned.

3 Remove detachable collars, cuffs and other trimmings which are washable.

4 Empty pockets.

5 Tack down pleats.

6 Brush well, inside and out.

7 Use moth-deterrent if necessary. Newspaper-lined containers will help to discourage moths.

8 Fold carefully and store in chests, cupboards or cases.

Avoid damp which can cause mildew by seeing that clothes are perfectly dry before storing. Avoid also the risk of moths laying eggs in garments. This usually happens on soiled portions or spots on garments, as the maturing larvae eat the dirty threads.

Preparing stored garments for wearing

1 Unpack and either fold up packing paper or destroy it.

2 Shake clothes and air well in fresh air if possible.

3 Press carefully, removing tackings from pleats.

4 Replace collars and other detached trimmings.

5 Hang clothes in wardrobe ready for use.

PREPARING GARMENTS FOR DRY-CLEANING

1 Empty pockets and turn inside out to remove fluff.

2 Remove any trimmings likely to be damaged by cleaning fluid, including buttons and buckles.

3 See that belt is securely attached.

4 Remove shoulder pads (some cleaning fluids have a destructive effect on the sponge-type pads).

5 Let down the hems at wrist and lower edge if you suspect that the garment may shrink during cleaning. (The pressed-in sleeve edge crease will be difficult to remove if the sleeve has to be let down after cleaning.)

6 Pin a note to the garment for the cleaner's benefit if any particular stain needs attention; say what caused the stain and approximately how long it has been there.

7 If you are going to use a coin-operated dry-cleaning machine at the laundrette, collect your garments together and weigh them. It is advisable to ask the attendant which day the cleaning fluid is changed as it will become extremely dirty by the end of its cycle.

Preparing garment for wearing after cleaning
1 Remove all cleaners' labels.
2 Air thoroughly to disperse the smell of cleaning fluid.
3 Replace buttons, shoulder pads, etc.
4 Re-press if necessary.
5 Hang garment in wardrobe ready for use.

REPAIRING GARMENTS

'A stitch in time saves nine' is an excellent proverb to remember. If a repair is made immediately it becomes necessary it can often be fairly simple, but if postponed complications generally arise. Wearing, washing and ironing will quickly enlarge a tiny slit into a lengthy tear, and a thin place into an extensive hole.

DRESS REPAIRS

Split Seams
Unpick sufficient of the stitching on each side of the split in the seam to provide thread for fastening off properly. Re-stitch the seam, beginning and ending 2·5 cm over the original stitching, in case the split was caused by a weak length of thread.

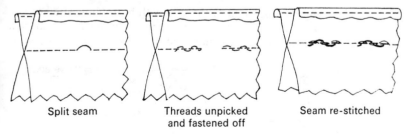

Split seam   Threads unpicked and fastened off   Seam re-stitched

Underarm Split

1 Unpick seams of sleeve and bodice as far as weakened portion extends.

2 Apply print patch (see p. 200) to worn sections, shaping unstitched edges to match those of the worn portions.

Note: Additional matching patch shapes are cut for the opposite bodice and sleeve, whether necessary or not, and for the back of the damaged side if not included in the repair, in order to resemble a gusset under both arms.

3 Re-stitch seams.

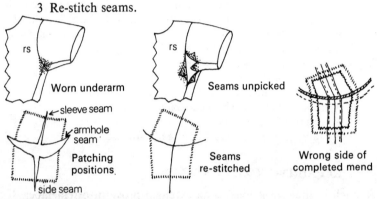

Worn underarm

Seams unpicked

Wrong side of completed mend

Patching positions

Seams re-stitched

Torn Dolman Sleeve

1 Trim frayed threads from split.

2 Undo seam for 2·5 cm at each side of split.

3 Cut triangle of matching material with two sides equal to the length of the split and with the base curved.

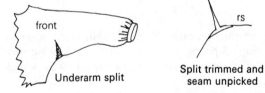

Underarm split

Split trimmed and seam unpicked

Shape of gusset

4 Strengthen the point of the split with buttonhole stitches.

5 Tack the right side of the gusset to the right side of the garment, sloping the stitches towards the point. Stitch gusset into slit as tacked.

Point of split neatened with buttonhole stitch

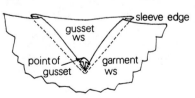

Gusset stitched into position

6 Press open the seam of gusset and garment.

7 Neaten all raw edges with loopstitch.

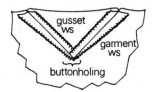

8 Make a cut into the back of sleeve to correspond with split in front and insert gusset in similar way.

9 Re-stitch the seam and press open.

10 Neaten the seam edges of the gusset.

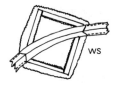

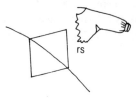

Corresponding gusset worked on back
of sleeve and seam re-joined

Completed gussets

Note: Even if undamaged the opposite sleeve must be treated in the same way.

Frayed Buttonholes

1 Cover existing buttonholes with decorative facing on the right side, contrasting if necessary. Darn back facing where necessary.

2 Re-work the buttonholes over original ones.

3 Work several rows of machine-stitching along edges of facing, to strengthen worn portions and disguise the repair.

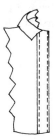

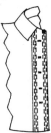

Three-cornered Tear

Work a hedge-tear darn as shown on p. 198, using threads drawn from the turnings of the garment.

Thin Place (e.g. at elbow of woollen dress or knitted cardigan/jumper) Work a thin-place darn as shown on p. 197, using matching darning wool or threads drawn from the turnings of the garment.

Split Pleat Seam (at point where seam ends and pleat hangs free, particularly on inverted pleats)

    1 Re-stitch broken seam.

    2 Work arrowhead over division for pleat to prevent future tearing and to disguise repair (see p. 78).

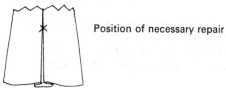

Position of necessary repair

Torn Pocket

Darn as for thin place and reinforce back of garment with a piece of lining or binding hemmed to the back.

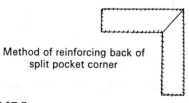

Method of reinforcing back of
split pocket corner

TROUSER REPAIRS

Worn Crutch on Trousers, Jeans or Pyjamas

    1 Unpick centre and leg seams on front and back to beyond the worn areas.

    2 Replace worn areas with a print patch (see *Underarm Split* p. 192) machined into place.

    3 Work a second line of machining 6 mm from the first to prevent the seam causing discomfort and to strengthen it.

    4 Re-stitch the seams, first the leg seams, then the crutch.

REPAIRS ON KNITTED GARMENTS

    1 Thin places, e.g. at elbows, need not become holes if mended in time—work thin-place darn large enough to cover entire worn part (as shown on p. 197).

    2 If holes have developed work a hole-darn as shown on pp. 197–8.

    3 Alternatively a large worn portion may be replaced by picking up a row of the stitches well below the damaged ones and wide enough to cover the entire breadth of the worn part, and knitting up a patch long enough to cover it. The worn portion is then carefully cut away, leaving

a row of loops along the top edge. The new piece is then grafted on to the garment along this edge (a good knitting book will give the necessary instructions for grafting) and the side edges are closed with a back-stitched seam.

REPAIRS TO UNDERWEAR

Broken Shoulder Straps

1 Carefully unpick stitches attaching the straps to the garment.

2 Attach new straps.

If the edge of a slip or nightdress has been damaged by the strain of the strap, it may be re-faced on the wrong side or a new decorative facing may be worked on the right side. Torn lace should be removed and a new edging attached.

Torn pointed fronts of slips may be re-cut to a different shape and neatened to match the rest of the edge.

Top of petticoat damaged by pulling away of shoulder strap

Top re-cut and shoulder strap replaced

Worn Underarms

1 Unpick side seam to 2·5 cm below damaged portion.

2 Insert shaped portion at each side of seam, using overlaid seam and cutting away worn parts. The insets should match in size and shape.

3 Re-stitch side seam.

4 Neaten top edge to match rest of edging.

5 Repeat process on other side of garment.

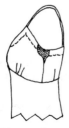
Worn underarm

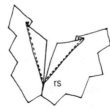
Seam unpicked and new portions inserted

Seam re-stitched

Wrong side of
repaired underarm

Torn Buttonholes at Waist (as on half-slips)
With Waistband

    1 Undo waistband 5–7·5 cm beyond buttonhole and cut off.

    2 Cut maching section from new material and join to old waistband. Press seam open.

    3 Replace waistband (see pp. 138–9).

    4 Work new buttonhole (see p. 42).

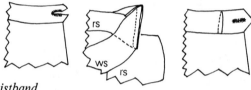

Without Waistband

    1 Cut off top of garment to depth of buttonhole or worn portion.

    2 Attach new band all round waist.

    3 Work new buttonhole.

cutting line

Torn Buttonholes on Openings

    1 Unpick existing opening.

    2 Re-work opening, using matching material.

    3 Attach new fastenings.

DARNING

Rules for all darns

    1 The thread used should match the garment in colour and texture, e.g. woollen yarn on woollen cloth, cotton thread on cotton material.

    2 Darning should be worked on the wrong side, selvedge (warp) direction first.

    3 The completed darn must be large enough to cover the hole and the surrounding worn parts.

4 An irregular shape should be worked to avoid strain on any one thread (except in the case of a hedge-tear where surrounding threads are not worn).

5 Loops should be left at the end of each row in order to allow the garment to stretch or the new threads to shrink without pulling the darn tightly.

6 Needle should be long enough to allow a whole row of stitches to be worked at once.

THIN-PLACE DARN

1 Work in a zig-zag shape to avoid strain on one thread.

2 Do not fasten thread on or off.

3 Tack shape in first if it is any help, although if the stitches are counted and the same number is worked in each row this should not be necessary.

4 To make the zig-zag shape, miss one stitch at the bottom of each row and work one stitch higher at the top for the upward slope and vice-versa for the downward one.

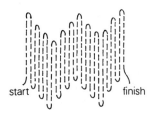

HOLE DARN

1 Remove frayed threads from the actual hole, leaving loops of knitted fabrics clearly visible round the edge.

2 Work the selvedge-direction threads first, forming an octagonal shape by working each of the first rows one stitch longer than the previous one, then a block of rows of equal length, and finishing with rows each decreasing in length by one stitch until the first number is reached.

3 The darn must be large enough to cover the hole and the thin place surrounding it.

4 Threads must be taken straight across the hole, picking up each loop to prevent laddering.

5 Repeat the same shape in the weft direction, weaving the weft threads over and under the selvedge ones. As they cross the hole the threads should fill it completely, with no spaces between them.

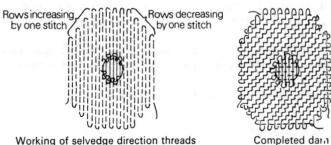

Rows increasing by one stitch   Rows decreasing by one stitch

Working of selvedge direction threads   Completed darn

Note: On small knitted garments (e.g. socks, gloves) a mould may be held under the portion to be darned—darning 'egg' inside socks, thimble inside glove finger.

HEDGE-TEAR DARN

The aim in working this darn is to make it as inconspicuous as possible. In order to achieve this result:

1 Draw the edges together without overlapping them, working fish-bone stitch with a hair to secure them.

2 Darn across the split (at right angles to it) in both directions, forming an L-shaped darn. For darning use threads drawn from the fabric of the garment so that the stitches are quite invisible.

As this shape is worked the weakest part of the tear (i.e. the angle where the two straight threads meet) is covered by a double darn. Work the stitches over 1·3 cm of the material at each side of the split and the same distance from each end.

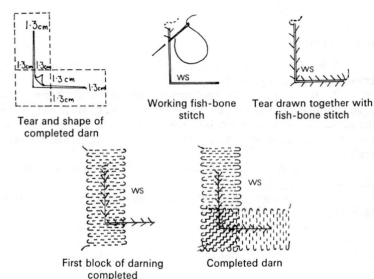

Tear and shape of completed darn

Working fish-bone stitch

Tear drawn together with fish-bone stitch

First block of darning completed

Completed darn

DARNING A CUT

This method is suitable for use on cut garments and on table linen and towels. On garments, matching thread should be used as for hedge-tear darns; on table linen fine darning cotton should be used; on towels, thicker darning cotton may be used. On garments, the edges should be drawn together with fish-bone stitch using a hair. On household articles fine cotton may be used.

Edges drawn together with
fish-bone stitch

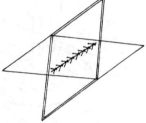

Shape of darn to be worked—
double line shows first block,
single line second block

The darn is worked first in the direction of the selvedge threads and then in that of the weft threads. The shape of the darn is made by working blocks of rows of equal length with the ends of the blocks parallel with the cut.

Working of first block of darning

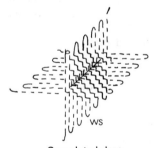

Completed darn

MACHINE DARNING

Method

    1 Fit the area to be darned into a small embroidery hoop. This is now provided with many modern sewing machines, but a small hand-embroidery hoop may be substituted providing it has an adjusting screw. The work should be right side up at the bottom of the hoop.

    2 Insert a new machine needle (it must be sharply pointed) one size finer than that normally used for the fabric being darned.

3 Thread the machine with the machine-embroidery cotton.

4 Drop or cover the feed on the machine.

5 Place the work under the machine and pick up the under thread through the fabric.

6 Lower the presser foot.

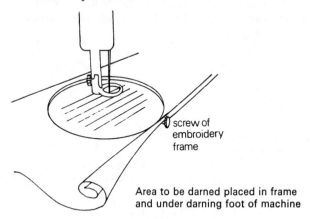

screw of
embroidery
frame

Area to be darned placed in frame
and under darning foot of machine

7 Holding the hoop firmly and keeping it down on the bed plate of the machine, move it backwards and forwards, covering the hole with rows of stitching as for hand darning.

Note: Keep the fingers out at the edge of the loop.

Common faults

1 Thread breaking: the hoop is being moved too fast for the speed of the machine.

2 Missed stitches: the hoop is being lifted off the machine as it is moved; or the needle is blunt.

PATCHING

PRINT PATCH

This is a useful method of repairing outer garments made of cotton, silk, rayon, linen and nylon. On printed or woven patterns it can be almost invisible.

Rules

1 The patching material must match that of the garment in pattern, colour and texture. New material used for patching should be washed if the garment has been washed, and gently bleached if the colour of the garment has faded. (Use chlorine bleaches for cottons only; use hydrogen peroxide for all fine fabrics.)

2 The patch should be cut perfectly square and large enough to cover the hole and all the surrounding worn part.

Method

1 Make a 1 cm turning on both sides of patch and then on top and bottom edges. Tack turnings into position.

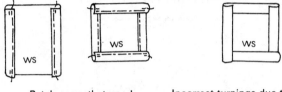

Patch correctly turned   Incorrect turnings due to folding
each side in turn round the patch

2 Tack patch over hole in garment, matching pattern exactly. (Pin in position with a pin across each corner before tacking, to ensure that patch does not slip.)

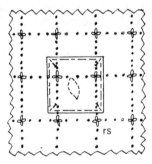

3 Turn back the garment along the top edge of patch, holding the patch side towards yourself. Oversew with tiny stitches along the two folds.

4 Work one stitch across the corner, unfold the garment and fold again along the second side of the patch, turning the work so that the edge to be stitched is at the top. Oversew second side.

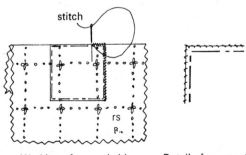

Working of second side   Detail of corner stitch

5 Repeat for third and fourth sides.

6 Remove tackings.

7 Turn to wrong side and cut garment material from the hole into each corner, stopping 1 cm from the stitches.

8 Cut turnings straight from corner to corner.

9 Loopstitch both edges together, taking care that the stitches do not go through to the right side and that one stitch is worked into each corner.

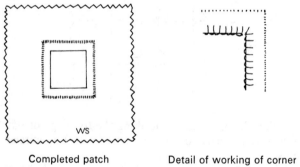

Completed patch   Detail of working of corner

COTTON OR CALICO PATCH

This patch is usually used for household mending—on sheets, pillow-cases, etc. A similar method may be used on cotton aprons, overalls and petticoats, where there is no pattern to be matched.

Rules

1 The patching material should match that of the worn article in colour, weave and age (new material sewn on to old fabric will often pull away the threads of the worn article).

2 The selvedge and warp threads of the patch must run in the same direction as those of the article to be mended.

3 The patch should be cut square in shape (straight to a thread on all sides) and be large enough to cover the hole and the surrounding worn part.

Method

  1 Make 1 cm turnings on both sides of the right side of the patch and tack them. Repeat on top and bottom edges.

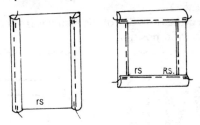

  2 Fold the patch in half in both directions and make creases along the fold lines.

  Fold the article to be patched in the same way, so that the creases would cross in the middle of the hole. Both creases should be as straight to a thread as possible.

Patch creased in both directions

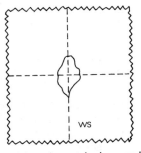

Article to be patched creased
to correspond with patch

  3 Pin the right side of the patch to the wrong side of the worn article, matching the creases. Tack along each edge, straightening the edge of the patch to a thread of the material if necessary.

  4 Hem all round the patch, taking care that a stitch is worked across each corner. Remove the tackings.

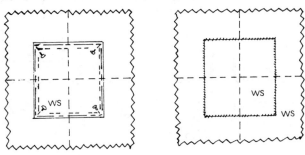

5 From the hole, cut into each corner of the stitching, stopping as the patch turning is reached. Cut turnings straight between the corners, 1·3 cm from the stitching lines. (This leaves 3 mm snip into the turning at each corner.)

6 Turn under the raw edge of the turnings from the snips at each corner. Tack and hem in position.

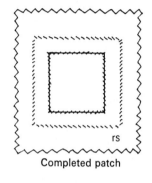

Shaded portion indicates portions cut away

Completed patch

BLANKET PATCH

This is the patch used for fabrics which are too bulky to turn under, for knitted materials, and for those which do not fray.

Method

1 Cut the patch to the required size, without turnings.

2 Apply patch to the right side of the article and fix into place with close 3-step zig-zag machine stitch or with herringboning, working over the raw edge.

3 Trim away worn fabric on the wrong side.

4 If herringboning has been used, work a second row over the raw edge on the wrong side, having cut down the turnings to 6 mm wide all round.

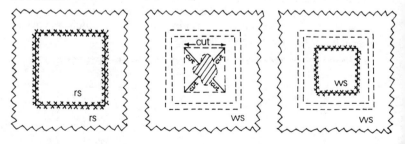

APPLIQUÉ/MOTIF PATCH

Apply the decorative motif to the right side of the garment over the worn area and stitch into place with satin stitch. The motif may be cut from suitable scrap material or embroidered or crocheted. Commercial motifs may be bought and some of these are fusible, merely requiring to be ironed on to the garment.

REPLACING TAPES, RIBBONS AND LOOPS

TAPES AND RIBBONS FOR TYING (See p. 32.)

HANGING LOOPS (latches/hangers made of tape, braid or rouleau)

First method
Each end is attached in the same way. Care must be taken that the tape is not laid flat on the garment or article.

    1 Make a turning which is a square of the width of the tape on each end of the piece.

    2 Pin each end into position, leaving some slack tape between them.

    3 Hem round three outside edges and backstitch fourth side of square, *or* machine around the square.

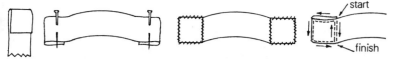

Preparation of tape   Attaching by hand   Attaching by machine

This method is suitable for latches for towels, coats, etc., and for slots for apron straps, etc.

Alternative method (for latches for towels or skirts)

    1 Fold tape in half widthwise and on one side oversew two edges together from the raw edges for twice the depth of the turning. (On wide tapes half the depth only may be turned under and this means that one and a half times the depth should be oversewn.)

    2 Flatten out the tape and turn up half the oversewn portion.

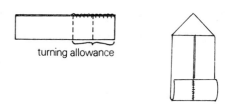

turning allowance

3 Place the tape against the edge of the article or garment as shown.

4 Hem round three sides of the turning and oversew the fourth side as shown, *or* machine the rectangle.

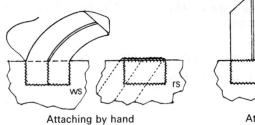

Attaching by hand   Attaching by machine

FURTHER STUDY

THINGS TO DO

1 Work specimens of the following processes and mount them. On attached slips suggest where these methods might be used and the garments for which they would be suitable.

a darns: thin place, hole, hedge-tear, cut

b patches: print, cotton

c attaching tape loops

d inserting a gusset in a dolman sleeve.

2 Repair a garment of your own, using an appropriate method.

3 Find out how to remove as many stains as possible from *a*. synthetic fibres and *b*. natural fibres.

4 Compare the cost of dry-cleaning a skirt, a pair of slacks, a woollen dress, a sweater and a coat *a*. commercially and *b*. in a launderette with an automatic dry-cleaning machine.

5 Find out the cost of commercial 'invisible mending'.

QUESTIONS TO ANSWER

1 Complete the following statements by filling in the blanks with words taken from the right-hand column:

a Cotton garments must be well-aired before storing as dampness may cause . . . . to develop.	right
b Woollen garments should always be washed or cleaned before putting away for any length of time, otherwise they may be attacked by	blanket
	zig-zag machine
c When garments are to be dry-cleaned in an automatic machine they must be . . . . as well as being prepared as for commercial cleaning.	loopstitch
	wrong

d In order to spread the strain on the threads a thin place is darned in a .... shape.

e A hedge-tear darn is worked in a .... shape as the surrounding threads are not usually worn.

f To ensure that the darning threads will not pull tightly on worn fabric and that they will 'give' with knitted threads, the lines of stitching have .... at each end.

g A print patch is applied to the .... side of the garment and is attached with ....

h A cotton patch is placed on the .... side of the article to be repaired and is held in place with ....

i A patch on a thick or knitted fabric is called a .... patch and may be applied with .... stitch or with .... stitch.

j Print patches are completed by trimming the raw edges on the wrong side and neatening them with ....

right-angle

mildew

oversewing

weighed

moths

zig-zag

hemming

herringbone

loops

2 What care should be given to school uniform consisting of a pinafore dress, blouse, cardigan and blazer *a.* every day and *b.* at intervals? Describe three repairs which may become necessary and give detailed instructions for carrying out *one* of them.

3 Why is it necessary for winter outfits to receive special care before being put away for the summer? Give details of the attention you would give before storing and the method of storage used for *six* of the following:

a a heavy woollen tweed coat

b a turtle-neck long-sleeve sweeter

c a worsted suit with a pleated skirt

d a velvet evening skirt

e a pair of fur-lined ankle boots

f a pair of fur-backed leather gloves

g a brown leather shoulder bag

h a brushed-nylon nightdress.

4 Household and clothing repairs are now very seldom worked but some are still necessary in the interests of thrift. What repairs are still carried out on *a.* household linen and *b.* personal clothing? How can an up-to-date sewing machine be used to advantage?

5 How would you prolong the use of:

a a cotton sheet which has worn thin in the middle?

b a pair of thin tea towels?

c a hand towel with frayed side edges?

 d a long-sleeved school blouse with a split elbow?

6 Describe, by means of diagrams and notes, the working of *two* of the following repairs:

 a the torn buttonhole on a child's woollen coat

 b the worn edge on the cuff of a sweater

 c a broken loop (hanger) at the neck of a coat

 d a thin place in a blanket.

7 How would you repair:

 a a three-cornered tear in the sleeve of a tweed jacket?

 b a hole in the finger of a knitted glove?

Illustrate your answers with diagrams showing all details.

8 Explain carefully how you would renovate a woollen dress which is badly worn at the elbows and underarm and threadbare at the collar.

9 How would you repair:

 a a woollen cardigan which has worn thin at the elbows?

 b a cotton dress, floral patterned, which has worn under the arms?

 c a school blazer in which one pocket has been torn away from the jacket at the top corner?

Illustrate your answer with diagrams.

10 How would you deal with:

 a paint on a woollen blazer?

 b a grass stain on a pair of white slacks?

 c oil on a light poplin raincoat?

 d blackcurrant juice on a linen tablecloth?

 e blood on a nylon blouse?

8

TEXTILES

Textiles which are used in needlework may be divided into two classes—
1 natural: *a* animal (wool, silk)
              b vegetable (cotton, linen)
2 'man-made': *a* regenerated (rayon)
                  b chemical (nylon, etc.)

The raw materials of which these cloths are made are known as fibres, and the characteristics of the finished fabric depend upon the fibre's degree of strength (both wet and dry), elasticity, absorbency, lustre, fineness and cohesion (i.e. whether or not the fibres bind well together).

WOOL

BRIEF HISTORY OF WOOLLEN CLOTH

Woollen garments can be traced back to the very earliest days of man's existence. In their most primitive forms they must have been simply the skins of the animals removed intact and very roughly cleaned, the rest of the animal providing food for the wearer.

In later days, when the process of spinning had been evolved, bunches of loose wool, caught on hedges and undergrowth as the animals passed, were collected, or plucked from the primitive breeds of sheep, and spun at home. Much of the cloth woven from this remained the rather dirty white of the original fibres, but some natural vegetable dyes were used and these gave subdued, rather drab colours. As these dyes were improved colours became more attractive, and it was these natural hues which were originally woven into the famous Scottish tartans.

During the Middle Ages England's prosperity was largely built upon the wool trade. The wool produced in this country was exported to the Continent for weaving. Many of the magnificent churches found in East Anglia and known as 'wool' churches are monuments to the merchants' prosperity. Later, Flemish weavers came to England and set up their trade in such places as Kersey and Worsted, which still give their names to the types of woollen cloth made there.

The very first factory for producing cloth in England, however, was founded much earlier than this, when the Romans set up looms for weaving warm cloth to protect their soldiers from the uncongenial and unfamiliar climate. This was at Winchester in the year A.D. 80. For many years now the woollen cloth trade in England has been centred in Yorkshire, the original factories having been opened in Bradford.

SOURCES

Woollen fibres manufactured into cloth in England come from Australia, New Zealand, South Africa, and the Argentine, which are the chief sheep-breeding countries.

TYPES OF FABRIC MANUFACTURED FROM WOOL

Woollen cloth: a close, warm-textured fabric made from raw and waste wool.
Worsted cloth: a finer, more handsome cloth made from new wool.
Wool jersey: machine-knitted from spun thread.
Felts: fine and coarse.
Pile fabrics: e.g. carpets.

CHARACTERISTICS OF WOOL FIBRES

1 The fibres are the natural hairs and wool of the sheep and vary in quality and length according to the breed (merino is the finest type). The shorter the fibres the finer they are, and they may range from 5–30 cm in length.

2 Each fibre is covered with overlapping scales but is not twisted. It is not a straight fibre, but has a wave or 'crimp' in it which gives wool threads their characteristic resilience. The scales, on the other hand, if interlocked by incorrect treatment, 'felt' the fibres together and destroy their elasticity.

Diagram of appearance of wool
fibres under microscope

3 Raw wool contains natural grease from the skin of the animal (from which lanolin is derived) and impurities such as dirt and burrs.
Advantages of natural wool fibres
1 The natural crimp of each fibre means that the spun threads hold well together and are firm to handle. Woollen cloth, on the whole, does not fray easily and knitting yarns do not readily divide.

2 Woollen cloth is warm to wear because the hairs on the wool strands hold tiny pockets of air which act as insulators. Wool is a good non-conductor of heat—i.e. there is no free passage of warm air from the body or of cold air from the atmosphere. Also, wool will absorb moisture very thoroughly, and this means that perspiration absorbed from the body evaporates very slowly and does not chill the body as it does so. When well-aired wool garments absorb moisture vapour from our damp winter atmosphere or from perspiration after exercise, the wool fibre generates heat, giving additional protection against cold.

3 The elasticity and resilience of the fibres make the finished cloth naturally crease-resisting. 'Sat-in' creases will drop out if the garment is hung up, and stubborn creases can be eliminated and shape regained with damp pressing. On the other hand, pressed-in creases will be well held, so woollen cloth is very satisfactorily pleated.

4 Woollen garments help to maintain body temperature.

5 Wool is non-inflammable—it smoulders, giving off a smell of burning hair. Therefore it is a safe material for children to wear.

6 Wool repels water-drops, owing to the natural oil in the fibres. Even after the processes involved in preparing it for weaving it will still shed light rain quite satisfactorily.

Disadvantages

1 When wet, the fibres become softened and will easily stretch if not controlled.

2 If incorrectly washed the scales of the fibres interlock and they become felted and matted. This causes the material to shrink and there is no remedy for this. The disadvantage can be exploited by the dressmaker when fullness on seams, particularly over the head of sleeves, requires shrinking. This is achieved by the application of a hot iron on the dampened material, hotter than that which would normally be used on wool. Commercial use is also made of this characteristic when flannel or baize is being manufactured (both very closely-bonded materials) or, in a modified degree, when lengths of cloth are pre-shrunk for cutting into garments.

Shrinkage of woollen cloth is brought about by:

a extremes of temperature

b rubbing when wet

c the use of alkalis (e.g. soda in water for washing).

For garments that need frequent cleaning, it is advisable to buy wool that has been treated for shrink-resistance and felting (Dylan) or has a machine-washable finish.

CARE OF WOOLLEN CLOTH

Knitted

1 Brush to remove loose dust (held by the hairy or fluffy surface).

2 Do not allow fabric to become too soiled, thus requiring drastic rubbing.

3 Wash in warm water and pure soap by kneading and squeezing the garment with the hands and avoiding rubbing. Rinse thoroughly in warm water.

4 Do not wring. Roll in a towel or give a short spin to remove surplus moisture.

5 Shape the garment gently while still damp.

6 Do not dry in direct heat.

7 Press lightly with a warm iron on the wrong side.

Woven

Have the garment dry-cleaned unless labelled as washable. All woollens should be protected from moths. This may be done by:

a making sure that no woollen garment is stored unless it is perfectly clean

b buying garments or fabrics with a moth-proof finish

c using a commercial moth-deterrent in the storing cupboard.

PRODUCTION OF WOOLLEN CLOTH

1 *Sorting:* the 'staples' (fibres) are sorted according to their length, soundness, colour and fineness.

2 *Scouring:* carried out in hot soapy water to remove the natural grease and sweat. (Lanolin is a by-product of this stage.)

3 *Rinsing and Drying*

4 *Carbonizing:* the immersing of the wool fibres in dilute sulphuric acid to enable the seeds and burrs, which become dry and powdery, to be crushed in later stages (wool is resistant to acid).

5 *Blending:* spreading different qualities of wool and waste in layers and passing them through a 'willeying' machine which opens out the fibres for carding.

6 *Carding:* the blending of the mixture and its conversion into a thin, soft band or 'sliver'.

7 *Combing:* (for worsted fabrics only) removing the short threads.

8 *Spinning:* the production of long threads by twisting the fibres together.

9 *Weaving:* the threads may be dyed before they are woven or after the fabric is completed. If several different dyed threads are used for weaving, a pattern is produced which is visible on both sides of the cloth and which will never deteriorate in wearing and cleaning. Gossamer-weight woollen cloth is made by twisting a fine yarn with a supporting thread for weaving. When complete, the support is removed from the cloth, leaving the fine web. Seaweed is often used to produce the supporting thread, and is later dissolved out.

Wool Materials

Flannel, tweed, mohair, merino, serge, hopsack, worsted, velour, felt, gaberdine, jersey, suiting, West of England cloth, Welsh flannel. Fabrics made of pure new wool bear the Woolmark. No other fibre may be added and no re-cycled wool used.

Wool Mixtures

Wool blends well with other fibres, e.g.:

rayon—to give a fabric that is cheaper than pure wool but not of such high quality;

cotton—to provide lightweight washable dress-weight fabrics such as Viyella and Clydella;

nylon—to give extra strength and resistance to abrasion;

terylene/courtelle—55% or more synthetic fibre gives drip-dry, washable fabrics that will hold permanent creases and pleats.

DIRECTIONS FOR SEWING WOOL

Cutting out

1 Shrink all wools which do not have a guaranteed shrink-resist, washable or machine-washable finish. (Press evenly all over on large, flat surface, using a hot iron over a damp cloth.)

2 Use sharp scissors. If fabric is very thick, cut one layer at a time.

3 Treat knitted wools, particularly single or weft knits and all loosely woven fabrics, very carefully when pinning on the pattern. These easily pull out of shape and the 'straight of the material' marking should be very accurately placed.

Tacking

Tack very firmly, using small, even tacking stitches.

Machining

1 Use sewing silk, when available, on all weights of wool cloth.

2 As an alternative use Sylko No. 50 on dress-weight wools and Sylko No. 40 on heavy skirt and coat-weight fabrics.

3 Use synthetic threads with care as these may disintegrate if the garment is subsequently pressed with too hot an iron.

4 On thick, knobbly wools lengthen the stitch to prevent the material from jamming under the presser foot. Use a medium heavy needle No. 16/90.

5 Use a fine needle, No. 14/80, on bouclé wools to pierce the knobbly threads easily.

Seaming

1 Use flat or open seams to reduce bulk.

2 Neaten these with zig-zag, 3-step zig-zag, overcasting or loopstitch.

3 'Step' or layer turnings on bulky fabrics to avoid too thick a

ridge where several turnings lie one over the other.

4 Sew 6 mm pre-shrunk binding tape to all seams on single-knit jersey fabrics to prevent stretching in wear.

5 Do not stretch bias seams.

Pressing

1 Shrink puckering or unwanted fullness from seams (e.g. over sleeve-head) by covering fullness with a damp cloth and holding a hot iron close above it. Finish by pressing lightly under a dry cloth.

2 Press all seams lightly over a damp cloth.

3 Damp ironed-in creases and re-press.

4 Press all wools on the wrong side.

SILK

BRIEF HISTORY OF SILK

Silk has a long romantic history which adds to the glamour always associated with it.

About 2600 B.C. silkworms were tended by royal hands and kept as a national secret in China. The stories of how silkworm culture spread westwards are numerous and varied. One theory is that a Chinese princess who married an Indian prince smuggled some silk-moth eggs out of China and taught the secrets of silk production to the people of India. This was about A.D. 550; but a conflicting tale is told of two Persian monks who, 1500 years ago, stole some silkworm eggs from China and brought them, hidden in their hollow bamboo pilgrim-staves, to Europe. Whatever the true story of the spread of silk production to the western world, it is undeniable that France and Italy soon became famous for their silk products. France's prosperity rested largely on her silk trade and when, in the nineteenth century, disease attacked the European stocks of silk-moths, both nations saw their prosperity threatened. Louis Pasteur was called in to advise the manufacturers but he knew nothing of this subject. He, in turn, consulted Henri Fabré and eventually Pasteur became so interested in his work that he laboured against the handicaps of illness and discouragement until he was able to conquer the disease.

SOURCES OF SILK FIBRE

The following countries have a climate suitable for sericulture on a commercial scale: Japan, Korea, China, Italy, India, Asia Minor, and Brazil. Iran, Turkey, Syria and the Lebanon, Greece and the Balkans all produce reeled silk from cocoons, and France's place in the silk world is now almost entirely concerned with the breeding of worms and the production of cocoons. England produces comparatively minute quantities of reeled silk.

SOURCES OF SILK CLOTH

Japan, South Korea, China, Italy and India produce beautiful fabrics. Iran's northern states are the contributory ones for the sericulture of the southern Soviet districts. France's contribution in this field is now not significant. England possesses very small silk-reeling and fabric-producing units for the home market.

CHARACTERISTICS OF SILK

1 The silk fibres are produced from the head of the silkworm as twin threads gummed together. Their natural use is as the cocoon for the silkworm. They are, therefore, extremely strong in spite of their fineness.

2 The threads have a natural lustre, as they have no twists in their original state. They therefore produce a beautiful fabric with a smooth, pearly sheen.

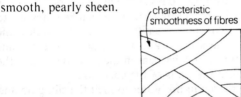

characteristic smoothness of fibres

Diagram of appearance of silk fibres under microscope

3 The fibres are naturally elastic and therefore crease-resistant.

4 Silk is warm to wear because it is a good non-conductor of heat. Moreover, it will easily absorb body moisture and does not allow the body to chill even when the material is wet.

5 Silk is an expensive fabric to buy, which is not surprising when it is estimated how many thousand silkworms are required to produce one kilogram of silk.

6 The fibres will readily absorb metallic salts which are often added to give weight and body to what is otherwise a very soft, light material.

7 Silk is non-inflammable: it forms a small soft ball when flame is applied and gives off a smell of burnt hair or feathers.

TYPES OF SILK

Silk: refers to the natural thread as it comes from the silkworm.

All silk: applied to fabrics which are unmixed with any other textile fibre (whether or not 'weighting' has been added).

Pure silk: where no weighting, except that introduced by the dyes, has been added.

Pure dye silk: no weighting of any kind has been introduced, even in the dye.

Spun silk: describes fabrics woven from the shortest lengths of waste silk produced during the spinning processes. These may vary from 2·5–20 cm, as compared with the natural lengths of silk threads which range from 350–1000 metres. Hence the somewhat 'bitty' surface of such material.

Silk Fabrics
Brocade, chiffon, taffeta, velvet, moiré, satin, shantung, surah, crêpe, georgette, organza, tussore, grosgrain, silk jersey.

PRODUCTION OF SILK

1 The silkworm is the grub of the silk-moth, which feeds entirely on mulberry leaves. The egg which the silk-moth lays is not larger than a pin-head, but when ready to spin its cocoon the caterpillar is from 7·5–10 cm long. It takes the creature two days and two nights of unceasing toil to spin enough silk to complete its cocoon, which requires up to 3 kilometres of thread. The filaments are emitted through two holes, one on each side of the caterpillar's head, and they emerge already surrounded by a gummy solution which hardens in the air and cements the twin threads together to form the walls of the cocoon.

2 The cocoons are placed in hot water to melt the silk gum and thus loosen the threads, and the surface is brushed to disclose the end of the thread.

3 The ends of the threads from several cocoons are placed together and unwound simultaneously, being twisted together as they unwind to form a thread of sufficient thickness to handle satisfactorily.

4 The twisted thread, still surrounded by the gum which has by now hardened again, is reeled into a skein. This is 'raw silk' and thirty of such skeins are folded together to be sent to the weavers.

5 Most of this raw silk is woven while still 'in the gum' and the gum is boiled away after weaving.

6 The waste silk is spun into threads in the same way as cotton or wool threads are spun.

7 Patterns may be introduced into silk fabric by printing them on to the completed cloth or during the actual weaving, when threads of various colours are used at the same time.

'Screen printing' is the method by which patterns are transferred to the cloth through silk stencils, one colour at a time. This is a very intricate operation and is a skilled and labour-intensive craft. Naturally this increases the price of the finished fabric, but it results in very beautiful colours and designs which are much more delicate than those achieved by mechanical processes.

CARE OF SILK

1 Test coloured silks for the fastness of the dye before washing.

(Press an inconspicuous portion of the garment over a damp cloth to see if the colour runs; if small cuttings of the material are available, wash and dry a piece for comparison with the original.)

If the colour is not fast, have the garment dry-cleaned.

2 Wash silk by kneading and squeezing it gently in warm, soapy water. Do not boil the fabric nor leave to soak before washing. Silk garments washed in a washing machine should be placed in a loosely woven bag for protection (an old pillowcase would be suitable).

3 Rinse thoroughly in warm water.

4 Remove excess moisture by rolling the garment in a towel and squeezing it.

5 Dry in the air, never before direct heat.

6 Iron on the wrong side while still slightly damp, using a warm iron, except for shantung and tussore which should be quite dry before ironing.

DIRECTIONS FOR SEWING SILK

Cutting out

1 Use very sharp scissors.

2 Do not allow for shrinkage.

Machining

1 Use fine needles, No. 11/70, and sewing-silk thread.

2 If fabric is very fine, machine over tissue paper to prevent it slipping and puckering.

3 Use a shorter than average length of stitch and adjust tension accordingly. Always test the tension on an odd scrap of material before working on the garment itself.

Seaming and Hemming

1 Use French or imitation French seams neatened with 3-step zig-zag to avoid fraying, tacking them carefully first.

2 Interface bottom hems with organdie if necessary to add weight and ensure good 'hang'.

3 Suitable stitches for neatening are 3-step zig-zag, zig-zag, machine edge-stitch, overcasting and loopstitch.

4 Carefully selected silk fabric is a good choice for long-life garments which can be handed on—e.g. wedding dresses, veils, christening robes, etc. It is not unrealistic, therefore, to use the more time-consuming hand finishes and decorative processes on this fabric.

Pressing

1 Use a warm iron—test on an odd scrap of material first as silk is easily scorched.

2 Press on the wrong side to avoid glazing.

Trimming

1 It is very difficult to find silk trimmings. Care must be taken that nylon laces and ribbons do not wear away the silk.

2 Match the quality of trimming to that of the silk so that both will wear at the same rate, e.g. fine cotton, rayon.

COTTON

BRIEF HISTORY OF COTTON

In addition to a great variety of clothing, cotton fibres also provide raw materials for such different goods as sails, book bindings, aircraft tyres, tents, candle-wicks, conveyor belts, bandages, etc.

Three thousand years ago Egyptian families cultivated the cotton plant and spun the fibres into threads for weaving. Cloth production then was carried out by very primitive means but the underlying principles were similar to those used in modern machine-production.

When the use of cotton spread to Europe and the Americas its history became associated with many of the darker pages of their stories. Slave labour in America was exploited for many years on the cotton plantations and in England young children were made to work for long hours in appalling conditions at the cotton mills.

Lancashire has long been the seat of the cotton-spinning industry in England, and here alone many million kilometres of thread are spun every week. The cotton fibres need a moist atmosphere to prevent them from becoming brittle during this operation and the humidity of the Lancashire climate is very suitable. Moreover, the ports are easily reached by ships bringing the cotton crops from America and other cotton-producing countries.

The quality of cotton varies according to its source, Egyptian cotton fibres being considerably finer than those grown in India, for instance.

SOURCES OF COTTON FIBRES

U.S.A., China, U.S.S.R., India, Egypt, Brazil, Mexico, Pakistan, Turkey, Sudan, Peru.

CHARACTERISTICS OF COTTON FIBRES

1 The cotton plant produces beautiful pink, red or white flowers and when, after a few days, the petals fall off, small round green pods remain. These are the seed pods of the plant and inside these the fluffy fibres grow from each tiny seed. The pods, or bolls, gradually become larger and eventually burst, revealing the mass of hair-like fibres. On modern plantations, the plants are often sprayed with defoliating chemicals to remove the leaves and allow the bolls to ripen more quickly.

As the cotton ripens, the fibres, which until now have been quite straight, twist themselves as shown in the diagram. The twist in the fibres means that they do not easily reflect light and most untreated cotton cloths (e.g. calico) have no lustre.

characteristic twist

Diagram of appearance of cotton
fibres under microscope

Advantages

1 Cotton fibres are stronger when wet than when dry. Cotton cloth is therefore quite safely boiled, wrung and scrubbed.

2 It absorbs dye readily and will take a variety of special finishes.

3 It is not damaged by alkalis (soda may therefore be used for softening the water in which cotton is washed, and for helping to clean greasy cotton cloths).

4 It readily absorbs moisture, which makes it very suitable for a clothing fabric.

5 It allows air to pass freely through its mesh, so making it a cool material to wear.

6 It is very hard-wearing even in its finest forms.

Disadvantages

1 Cotton fibres have little resilience and therefore materials made from them are apt to crease badly, unless treated with a crease-resistant finish. The poorer qualities are also somewhat stiff to handle.

2 It soon becomes saturated with moisture and, unless specially treated, has no waterproof qualities.

3 If stored while damp it is inclined to develop mildew.

Cotton garments to be stored for any length of time must be thoroughly aired first.

4 Vegetable fibres are inflammable, burning with a smell of scorched paper.

5 Loosely woven cloths may shrink when washed. Allowance must be made for this when making up garments.

CARE OF COTTON MATERIALS

1 Soak badly soiled articles in cold water to which a biological detergent or soaking powder has been added.

2 Wash coloured cottons in hot, soapy water and rinse in cold water. (Most dyed cottons nowadays are colour-fast but, if colours are inclined to run a little, vinegar may be added to the rinsing water to reduce the loss.)

3 White cottons may be boiled to improve their colour.

4 Unless specially treated and labelled, most untreated cotton goods are improved by passing them through a starch solution before ironing them. Organdies and voiles do not require this—if ironed while damp they recover their original crispness.

5 Unless the finish of the material requires special attention (e.g. embroidery must be pressed on the wrong side), cottons may be ironed on the right or wrong side, using a hot iron.

Note: As cotton is strong when wet, garments may be pulled into shape while still damp to facilitate ironing.

SPECIAL FINISHES OF COTTON

These are indicated on the label attached by the manufacturer, and care must be taken to treat the fabrics accordingly.

Crease-resisting: the fibres are impregnated with a chemical so that the cotton recovers from creasing in the same way that wool, being a naturally resilient fibre, does naturally. Crease-resistant cottons do not hold pleats.

Permanent glaze: the surface of this cloth should not be rubbed during washing. It is advisable to test a small portion of the fabric before ironing to see whether the best results are obtained by pressing on the right or wrong side.

Non-iron: do not wring this material after washing. Pull into shape, hang and allow it to drip-dry.

Embossed: wash gently and press under a dry cloth with a hot iron.

Trubenized: this material is permanently stiffened and requires no starching. It should be pressed with a hot iron while very damp.

Sanforized: the cloth is shrunk before appearing on the market and therefore no allowance for shrinkage need be made.

Mercerized: the threads have their twists removed by passing them through caustic soda solution and so acquire a lustre.

PRODUCTION OF COTTON CLOTH

1 *Ginning:* the raw cotton is passed through a machine which separates the seeds from the fibres and removes most of the rest of the pieces of plant which may have become entangled with them.

2 *Baling:* the packing of the cotton lint into bundles for shipping to the factories.

3 *Bale breaking:* at the spinning mills the bales are fed into machines which break down the matted fibres and rid them of impurities.

4 *Opening and cleaning:* continuing the breaking down and cleansing processes and producing an unbroken sheet of cotton fibres, known as a 'lap'.

5 *Carding:* separating the fibres and removing the short threads. This process produces a loose rope of cotton fibres known as a 'sliver'.

6 *Combing:* laying the fibres side by side by passing the slivers over revolving drums set with teeth.

7 *Drawing:* pulling out or 'drawing' the slivers and twisting several into one. Repeated several times.

8 *Slubbing:* further drawing into a thin sliver, now called a 'roving', and winding the rovings on to bobbins (this twists the thread slightly).

9 *Roving:* drawing out a single thread fine enough for spinning.

10 *Spinning:* the further drawing out and twisting of the threads into a continuous length for weaving.

11 *Winding:* removing faults in the threads and winding them on to larger and more convenient reels.

12 *Doubling:* twisting together two or more threads for greater strength.

13 *Weaving:* the passing of weft threads alternately over and under warp ones on a loom.

14 *Printing:* passing the completed cloth through rollers which print on pattern and colour, one colour at a time. Cottons may also be screen printed and very intricate designs achieved.

Cotton Fabrics

Calico, cambric, seersucker, gingham, voile, sateen, sailcloth, net, organdie, denim, cretonne, corduroy, piqué, towelling, velveteen, twill, chintz, gaberdine, crêpe, crepon, plissé, velvet, awning.

Warning: Many cotton fabrics which appear to have a good finish and sufficient body to give good wear while still being cheap, have been bolstered with a certain amount of stiffening dressing. When this is washed out in the first laundering of the material, it leaves the threads limp and thin. To test whether a fabric contains dressing, rub two surfaces together; if dressing is present a fine white powder will fly from the surfaces.

DIRECTIONS FOR SEWING COTTON

Cutting out

1 Do not attempt to tear haircords or seersuckers in order to straighten the ends.

2 Allow for shrinkage on loosely woven or dressed cottons.

Machining

Use cotton or Sylko sewing threads.

Seaming

1 Use French or open seams according to the type of garment and the position of the seam.

2 Neaten all raw edges.

Pressing

1 Use hot iron, on right or wrong side as required. Resin-glazed fabrics should be ironed on the wrong side only.

2 Damp out ironed-in or fold creases.

Trimming

Use cotton ribbons, laces, etc., matching the style and weight of the garment and its decoration.

LINEN

BRIEF HISTORY OF LINEN

Linen was well known to the countries of the ancient world. Wall-paintings in Egyptian tombs show the cultivation of flax for linen four thousand years ago, and actual linen mummy-cloths which must be six thousand years old are still to be seen in museums.

In England the first linen-manufacturing centre was set up in Winchester to supply the Roman army of occupation with clothing material. When they left, the manufacture of linen was carried on as a domestic industry and in the fourteenth century a guild of linen weavers was established in London. The first skilled weavers were those who came to England from Flanders.

Flax-growing was encouraged by an act passed in the sixteenth century, stipulating that a proportion of all agricultural land should be sown with flax and hemp seed. In the seventeenth century flax-growers were further encouraged by the offer of bonuses, and imported linen cloth was taxed. In spite of these efforts, however, flax and linen production did not flourish in England, and nowadays Northern Ireland is the only part of the British Isles known for its flax-growing, although there are some linen-producing firms in Scotland.

Linen is widely used for naval and industrial canvas owing to its great strength when wet, as well as for damask table-linen, tea and glass cloths, fine embroidery cloth and dress fabrics.

SOURCES OF FLAX

U.S.S.R., Poland, Belgium, France, Netherlands.

CHARACTERISTICS OF LINEN FIBRES

The threads are produced from inside the stems of the flax plant, where they appear in the form of smooth, strong, non-fluffy fibres held together by a natural gum.

characteristic nodes

Diagram of appearance of linen
fibres under microscope

Advantages

1 Linen is very strong, although a little more brittle than cotton. When wet it is even stronger than when dry.

2 It is smooth to the touch and therefore cool to wear (no warm air is trapped) and not easily soiled.

3 It absorbs moisture well (better than cotton but not so well as wool) and is suitable for underwear and other garments.

4 It has no fluffy surfaces and does not produce them even after repeated washings and rubbings.

5 It withstands high degrees of heat and is not affected by alkalis; therefore it may be boiled, washed in water containing soda, and ironed with a hot iron.

6 It is firm to handle and will give good tailored results.

Disadvantages

1 Linen has little resilience and therefore creases badly unless specially treated to become crease-resistant.

2 Expensive.

3 Being so smooth-textured, loosely woven linens are inclined to fray easily.

4 It will develop mildew if stored in an airless place while damp.

5 It is inflammable.

CARE OF LINEN FABRICS

1 Most linen fabrics may be washed, using hot water, hard soap and soda if necessary (i.e. on greasy garments).

Discoloured linens may be bleached (with chlorine bleach) if necessary but if it is well washed and dried in the sun white linen will remain a good colour.

2 Rinse thoroughly in cold water.

3 Starch if necessary—good linens have a natural crispness which renders this unnecessary.

4 Iron on wrong side (unless a glazed finish is required) with a hot iron while still damp.

5 Roll table-linen for storing, to avoid yellowing at crease-marks.

PRODUCTION OF LINEN CLOTH

1 *Retting:* the rotting away of the woody covering of the flax stems. In earlier times the bundles of stems were soaked in ponds which were specially dammed for the purpose. Nowadays this process is carried out in tanks under controlled conditions.

2 *Scutching:* the cleaning of the fibres, freeing them of seeds and stem-covering.

3 *Hackling:* the combing out and straightening of the fibres, incidentally removing the short threads or tow. The fibres are then formed into a sliver.

4 *Spinning:* the sliver is passed through a trough of hot water to loosen the natural gum on the fibre and to facilitate the twisting together of several strands to produce a compact yarn.

5 *Weaving:* many linens are produced in plain weave but the beautifully patterned damask tablecloths are woven on the jacquard loom.

6 *Bleaching:* loomstate linen cloth is off-white, fawn or greyish in colour. For white and coloured cloth this must be bleached. If colour-woven patterns are required this bleaching and dyeing is carried out at the yarn stage.

7 *Printing:* printed patterns are applied to the cloth after weaving, but much of the beauty of linen for table use lies in the intricate damask patterns which are woven into the cloth.

Linen Fabrics
Damask, crash, sheeting, towelling, dress-, suit- and coat-weight plain-weave fabrics, either 100% linen or linen/polyester blends.

DIRECTIONS FOR SEWING LINEN

Making up
Assemble the garment as soon as possible after cutting out and handle as little as possible to avoid fraying.

Machining
1 Use needle of suitable size for the weight of the fabric.

2 Use pure silk, Sylko sewing thread or good quality sewing cotton.

Seaming
1 Use open seams to reduce bulk and neaten all raw edges.

2 Use 3-step zig-zag or stretch stitch to neaten armhole and waist seams where friction could fray loosely-woven linens.

Pressing
1 Use hot iron.

2 Press on wrong side to avoid glazing.

3 Do not allow fabric to become too crumpled during making-up. Linen, unless specially treated, creases easily and too frequent pressing will reduce newly made freshness.

RAYON

SHORT HISTORY OF PRODUCTION

Over fifty years ago the shiny, brittle fabrics which were produced were known as 'artificial silks', but they actually bore very little resemblance to true silk except in lustre. Today, the quality and variety of fabrics which have been evolved are so much improved that rayon is valuable on its own merits, and not as a cheap substitute.

Rayon fibres are produced by chemical means from natural sources. The basis of all these fibres is cellulose, either from wood-pulp or cotton lint, and this is regenerated into:

a viscose rayon
b cellulose acetate rayon
c triacetate rayon
d modified rayon

Viscose Rayon

This is a widely used fibre, and is produced by converting the cellulose (usually wood-pulp) into a viscous solution by means of the action of caustic soda and then carbon disulphide. The solution is then wet spun by forcing it through tiny holes (spinnerets) into an acid which coagulates the fluid into continuous threads or filaments.

After washing, drying, bleaching and removing the sulphurous deposits the fibres are ready for weaving. Sometimes the filaments are divided into short, equal lengths and spun into yarn (as for cotton yarn) before weaving. These threads, when made into cloth, are known as 'spun rayons'.

Cellulose Acetate Rayon

This is a chemical compound of cellulose and acetic acid. The cellulose used is usually cotton linters, which is treated with acetic anhydride and acetic acid, mixed with a little sulphuric acid. The cellulose compound formed is dissolved in acetone (similar to nail-varnish remover) which evaporates when the fluid is forced through spinnerets into a chamber of warm air. This is known as dry spinning. The filaments thus formed are then ready for weaving.

Cellulose acetate rayons are more expensive than viscose rayons, but are of a high quality.

Advantages

1 As it is an artificially produced fibre, many different finishes may be introduced, e.g., dull or lustrous, fine or coarse, napped or smooth, crease-resisting, etc.

2 Viscose rayon is an absorbent fibre, therefore cool to wear. If cut into lengths and bulked for spinning (staples) before weaving, the finished cloth is warmer (mesh more easily traps warm air).

3 It takes dye well and blends well to produce rayon/cotton or rayon/wool mixtures. White rayon remains white.

4 It absorbs moisture fairly well, and is therefore suitable for underwear. Acetate rayons may be treated to repel moisture.

5 It is soft to handle, drapes and wears well.

6 It is reasonably priced and attractive.

Disadvantages

1 Rayon is much weaker when wet than when dry. It should not,

therefore, be wrung, twisted or stretched when wet.

2 It has little resilience and therefore creases badly unless specially treated.

3 Acetate rayon cannot withstand heat. When flame is applied the thread burns and melts, setting hard immediately afterwards. Viscose rayon burns as cotton.

Acetate rayon is thermoplastic, i.e. it softens on heating, it melts and at 230 °C it decomposes. Therefore these fibres have a high fire risk when used for children's clothes and nightwear.

4 The thread is very smooth and therefore cloth frays readily.

5 When wet, rayon becomes harsh to handle, however soft it is in its dry state. This is the exact opposite of the effect of moisture on silk.

Triacetate Rayon

Cellulose triacetate was, in fact, the first rayon to be produced but at the time when it was discovered the solvents which were available were too dangerous to use. With the development of methylene dichloride as a solvent it is possible for triacetate fibres to be dry spun, i.e. the solvent is evaporated into the air.

Advantages

1 It is thermoplastic, i.e. it can be heat-set into permanent pleats and creases in the same way as synthetic fibres.

2 It has a higher melting point than acetate, nylon or terylene.

3 It is resistant to boiling water and does not lose its sheen when in contact with it.

4 It is resistant to creasing, shrinking and stretching.

5 It dries quickly and requires little ironing.

6 It is similar in appearance to cellulose acetate but it washes and wears better.

Disadvantages

1 Although it shrinks and melts like synthetic fibres it also burns and flares like other rayons.

2 It has a tendency to become electro-statically charged.

3 It is less absorbent than natural fibres and viscose rayon. Lingerie fabrics made of triacetate, therefore, should be of jersey or warp knit construction.

On the other hand it has some 'wicking' properties, i.e. if it is used as a lining to garments made of cotton or other absorbent fabric, moisture from the skin passes through to the absorbent layer. This property is used to advantage in the production of certain napkins for babies, when a triacetate rayon layer is worn next to the skin and does not hold urine in contact with it. This can prevent chaffing and soreness, particularly when the baby's napkin cannot, for various reasons, be changed immediately it becomes wet (e.g. on long journeys).

Modified Rayon

Sarille: a staple rayon which is crimped to give it a natural warmth. It may be blended with polyester.

Vincel: this rayon is claimed to be the man-made fibre nearest in characteristics to cotton, having greater wet strength than other rayons. It is produced as fabrics similar to traditional cotton materials, particularly jersey, and is also blended with cotton. However, it is not so hardwearing as cotton.

Rayon Fabrics

Crêpe, ninon, taffeta, velvet, sharkskin, gaberdine, jersey, satin, net.

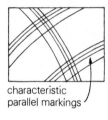

Diagram of appearance of rayon fibres under microscope

characteristic parallel markings

CARE OF RAYON

1 Read and obey the instructions on the label attached to the material or garment.

2 Wash in moderately hot, soapy water or as specified on the label.

3 Rayon may be machine washed, following the manufacturer's instructions regarding length and temperature of wash.

4 Triacetate rayons: permanently pleated garments should be hand-washed and dried. As this fibre is thermoplastic, care should be taken to ensure that it is cold rinsed before being spun dried, otherwise it may acquire permanent creases, giving it a rough-dry appearance.

5 Iron on the wrong side with a moderate iron.

DIRECTIONS FOR SEWING RAYON

Cutting out

1 Tear a strip off the end of the piece of the fabric to straighten the end.

2 Pin at close intervals to prevent material from slipping under the pattern.

3 Cut with very sharp scissors.

4 Do not allow for shrinkage.

5 To prevent fraying make up as soon as possible after cutting out.

Seaming

1 Use fine, sharp needles and pins.

2 Use French seams on fine and lightweight fabrics. Ensure that there are firm neatenings when plain seams are used on thicker rayons that are likely to fray badly, e.g. imitation linens, brushed rayons and some sarilles. Allow good turnings on hems.

Machining

1 Sew with Drima, Trylko or Sylko according to the weight of the fabric.

2 Sew over tissue paper with a fine needle, if fabric is very thin.

Pressing

1 Use cool or warm iron (test on odd scrap of fabric first), on right or wrong side according to the surface.

2 As there is such a wide variety of rayons on the market, always test a spare piece of the fabric before damp-pressing a garment. On some types produced as imitation silks this may cause a watermark.

Trimming

Cotton, nylon or rayon lace and ribbon may be used.

NYLON

OUTLINE OF PRODUCTION

Nylon is the name applied to the polyamide group of fabrics which were originally produced in America in the late 1930's. They were regarded as phenomenal materials when they first appeared and their versatility allows nylon to be adapted to form textile yarns, bristles, hinges, household utensils, screws, ropes, and many more unlikely articles.

The raw materials from which nylon is produced are coal, air and water, which go through several chemical changes to produce a nylon salt. This in turn is converted into nylon polymer, a cloudy-white substance resembling chips of marble. The polymer chips are fed into a hopper from where they are passed into a heating system which reduces them to a molten state. This fluid is then forced out through spinnerets and the resulting filaments are cooled by a current of air.

The fibres are then 'cold drawn', that is, they are stretched out to four times their original length, giving the yarn a certain amount of elasticity and increased strength. The resulting thread is wound on to spools, ready for weaving, or is cut into staples for twisting, as rayon thread is for spun rayon.

Diagram of appearance of nylon
fibres under microscope

Advantages

 1 Like rayon, nylon may be produced in a great variety of textures, thicknesses and finishes.

 2 It is extremely strong when dry.

 3 It is nearly as strong when wet.

 4 It has great elasticity and resilience, therefore resists and sheds creases.

 5 It is very smooth and is not roughened by rubbing.

 6 It does not shrink.

 7 It dries very quickly—water-resistant.

 8 It is resistant to moths and mildew.

 9 It may be satisfactorily blended with wool, cotton, rayon, flax or other man-made fibres.

 10 It is thermoplastic and therefore may be set into permanent creases or pleats.

Disadvantages

 1 Nylon does not absorb moisture, therefore it is not entirely suitable for underwear unless woven as a cellular fabric, which allows the passage of air and encourages evaporation.

 2 It is very smooth and slippery to handle and frays easily.

 3 It is a non-conductor of heat and therefore, unless woven as a mesh, hot to wear.

 4 It is damaged by heat—it melts and retreats from the flame, forming a bead, and gives off a smell of celery.

 5 White nylon gradually becomes greyish or yellow.

 6 Charges of static build up in the fibres, causing fabrics to cling to other clothing and to attract dirt. Anti-static types of nylon are being developed.

 7 The fibre is strong and when it 'pills' during wear these little nubs of fibre cannot be brushed off as they can from wool.

 8 As it is thermoplastic fibre, care must be taken to cold rinse before spinning dry, to avoid unwanted permanent creases.

CARE OF NYLON

 1 Read labels attached to fabrics for special instructions.

 2 Wash in warm, soapy water and rinse well.

 3 Iron on wrong side using a barely luke-warm iron. Test a sample of the material for the correct heat of iron whenever possible.

 4 Do not dry over or in front of direct heat.

 5 Roll in a towel to remove surplus moisture and dry completely in a current of air.

Nylon Fabrics

Satin, net, jersey, warp knit, proofed nylon, seersucker, plissé.

DIRECTIONS FOR SEWING NYLON

Cutting out
1 Leave good turnings to allow for fraying.
2 Do not make allowance for shrinkage.
3 Do not try to tear the fabric.
4 Use very sharp scissors.

Machining
1 Use Trylko, Drima, Guttermann, Molyneke.
2 Use very fine needles, Nos. 9/60–11/70.
3 Use loose rather than tight tension and a shorter than average stitch on fine fabrics.
4 Do not stretch the fabric as it is passed through the machine. Practise on a cutting of the material before stitching the garment.

Seaming
1 Never leave raw edges—use French seams stretch stitched and 3-step zig-zag seams on transparent woven fabrics.
2 Sew warp knit, jersey or stretch fabrics with stretch stitch if an automatic swing-needle machine is available, or on a slight zig-zag, bight $\frac{1}{2}$–1, on a swing-needle machine.
3 On transparent materials make sure that all seams are of the same width and neaten them carefully.
4 See p. 127 for method of attaching collar.

Turnings
Make hems double (i.e. two turnings of the same depth) to prevent frayed edges looking untidy inside the hems.

Pressing
1 Test first on a scrap of the same material.
2 Use medium-warm iron.
3 Press seams under a dampened cloth.

Trimming
Trim nylon garments with nylon lace and ribbon, so that all parts of the garment dry and wear at the same rate.

OTHER SYNTHETIC FIBRES

POLYESTER FIBRES

The first of the polyester fibres, Terylene, was discovered in 1941. These fibres are based on petroleum products—ethylene glycol and terephthalic acid—and are produced in many forms. In the textured filament form, Crimplene, it is suitable for a large range of clothing. Staple yarns may be blended with worsted, cotton and rayon.

Characteristics
Polyester fibres are versatile and may be blended with natural fibres. If there is a high percentage of synthetic fibre the resulting fabrics retain

much of the appearance of the traditional materials but have added easy-care properties.
Fabrics: jersey, lawn, suiting.

ACRYLIC FIBRES

The first of these, Orlon, was developed in the U.S.A. and was followed by its British counterparts Acrilan and Courtelle. These fibres are based on the chemical acrylonitrile which is made from petroleum products or natural gas. They are produced as staple fibres only in Britain and can be blended with wool and sometimes with cotton fibres.
Characteristics
Of all the synthetic fibres, the acrylics are those which most nearly resemble wool in softness and warmth of handle.
Fabrics: tweed, jersey, fleece, simulated fur.

MODACRYLICS

This group of fabrics have many of the characteristics of the acrylic group with the added advantage of flame-resistant properties. Unlike other synthetics this group does not melt or drop when in contact with flame. The British development is Teklan.
Fabrics: fleece, simulated fur.
Each year new developments appear in the field of man-made fibres. For the latest information—there will have been advances even before this book is produced—consult the booklet *Facts About Man-made Fibres* which is published annually and is available from: British Man-made Fibres Federation, Bridgewater House, 58 Whitworth Street, Manchester M1 6LS.

FURTHER STUDY

THINGS TO DO

1 Find a teazle and discover what its connection was with cloth-making.

2 Look round churches in your district and find memorials or other pictorial representations of the clothes of other periods. Make rubbings of any brasses showing interesting garments.

3 Boil a small piece of white cloth (preferably with some wool content) with onion skins. Note the result and compare it with that produced by boiling similar pieces with various berries and mosses.

4 Find as many surnames as you can which denote that originally the owner was occupied in some aspect of the clothing trade (e.g. Fuller —a fuller was engaged in 'fulling' or cleaning cloth).

5 Find passages in literature referring to people working with or on cloth in some way.

6 Find answers to the following questions:

a In the animal world what creatures spin and which ones weave?

b Who was the Greek patron goddess of weaving?

c Who was the patron saint of spinners?

d Why was a Spinning Jenny so important?

e Why did unmarried women become known as 'spinsters'?

f What is Spitalfields?

g Who were the Merchants of the Staple?

h The word 'strive' means to try hard. What is a 'striver' in lace-making?

i Why did a knight wear a surcoat over his armour?

j What is the real meaning of a 'masterpiece'?

k Which cathedral has a picture on the door of a woman spinning?

l Why did an Act of 1684 decree that 'all corpses must be buried in woollen shrouds'?

7 Collect samples of as many different fabrics as possible, with prices. Classify them according to their fibres.

Mount a specimen of each, giving name, nature, price, width and an example/illustration of suitable garments for its use. Mention any special care required in making up, pressing, laundering, or general maintenance.

8 Collect samples of pure wool, silk, cotton, linen, rayon and nylon.

a Make microscopic slides of the fibres of each and draw their appearance.

b Burn threads of each and identify the characteristic smells.

9 Make a study of the care of different fabrics (e.g. wool cloth, worsted, jerseys, lawn, nylon, rayons, terylene, silk, linen, cottons—different weights, colours, finishes, blends of each). First cut ten squares (approx. 6 cm × 6 cm) of each and either label them or keep them in separate envelopes.

Prepare a squared chart on which to mount your specimens, making each square of your chart 2 cm wider and deeper than the squares of fabric.

Mount one square from each of the different fabrics under the heading 'Original Fabric'. Mount each of the other squares in turn, having treated one of each set as follows:

a wash with detergent

b wash with soap flakes

c hot rinse

d cold rinse

e soak in chlorine bleach

f soak in soda water

g press with hot iron when dry

h press with hot iron when wet

i wash, dry, damp down and press.

Draw up a set of conclusions as to correct treatment of each fabric.

10 Visit a factory in which fabric is made, or a museum or exhibition which shows the manufacture, and write an account of what you see.

QUESTIONS TO ANSWER

1 Complete the following statements by filling in the blank spaces with words taken from the right-hand column:

Section A

a The animal fibres used for textiles are .... and	rayon
b The vegetable fibres which are used for textiles are .... and	scales
c A regenerated fibre used for textiles is	insulator
d The finest type of wool staple comes from .... sheep.	silk
e If incorrectly treated wool fabric will shrink because its .... interlock.	pleats
f Wool is a warm fabric to wear because its fibres trap a layer of air which acts as an	linen
g The elasticity of wool fibres give fabric a .... quality although it will hold .... well.	merino
	wool
	crease-resisting
	cotton

Section B

a When raw wool is scoured the natural grease is removed and used as .... for the basis' of various cosmetics.	retting
b The long, thin, soft band of fibres produced by carding is called a	weighting
c When wool is blended with cotton before being woven, a fabric known as .... is produced.	felting
d Wool fibres may be made into fabric by ...., ... or	Viyella
e Metallic salts are sometimes added to silk	flax
	weaving

fabrics to give them body, and this process is known as .... | sliver

f Fabric which is produced from short lengths of silk thread is called .... silk. | spun

g Linen threads are obtained from the .... plant. | lanolin

h The woody covering of the plant stems are rotted away by immersion in water; this process is called .... | knitting

Section C

a Cotton fibres are produced from the seed pods or .... of the cotton plant. | Trubenized

b Unlike silk, cotton fibres are twisted and therefore have no natural .... | tri-acetate

c Cotton fibres can be chemically straightened and are then said to have been .... | ginning

| bolls

d Untreated cottons can shrink when wet but if purchased as .... they can be safely washed. | sanforized

e Cotton fabrics can be permanently stiffened and are then labelled as .... | lustre

f .... is the removal of seeds and other waste matter from the cotton fibres before they are prepared for spinning. | regenerated

| hackling

g When raw cotton fibres are straightened and laid side by side the process is known as ....; the similar process using linen threads is called .... | mercerized

| combing

h Because rayon is made from cellulose produced by breaking down vegetable matter, the material is called a .... fibre.

i The first rayon to be developed was .... rayon.

Section D

a Fabric which can be heat-set into shape (e.g. into pleats) is described as being .... | weaker

b .... is a rayon fabric closely resembling cotton. | polyamide

c The best threads for sewing man-made fibres are .... and .... | filament

d The chemical name for nylon fibres is .... | stronger *e* When cotton is wet it is .... than it is when it is dry, rayon is .... and wool is ....

f A long, smooth, continuous fibre is called a ....

g Rayon and other man-made fibres are produced by passing the molten material through ....

thermoplastic

spinnerets

Drima

weaker

Trylko

Vincel

Section E

a The raw materials from which nylon is produced are ...., ... and ....

b Orlon is an .... fibre and is the .... original of the .... Acrilan.

c The granules from which nylon thread is produced are known as nylon ....

d The basic raw material of Crimplene is ....

e The effect of .... treatment on fabrics is to make them flame-resistant.

f Wool with a .... finish is shrink and felt resistant.

petroleum

Proban

American

polymer

acrylic

water

Dylan

coal

British

air

2 Name four different fabrics used in dressmaking today. Give the source of the fibres from which each is made and describe exactly the precautions required when pressing each fabric. Give your reasons.

3 Design a school uniform consisting of three different garments. State the fabric and colour you would choose for each and say why you have chosen each material.

4 What do you understand by *a*. blended fibres and *b*. mixtures of fibres? What advantages are there in combining (*i*) cotton with terylene, (*ii*) wool with nylon and (*iii*) worsted with viscose?

5 What advantages have the following fabrics as clothing materials?

a nylon jersey

    b Crimplene

    c worsted suiting

    d cotton seersucker

    e bonded terylene.

What disadvantages have you found in sewing *one* of these?

    6 What do you understand by 'synthetics'? Name four such fabrics and assess their value in (*i*) ease of working, (*ii*) washability, (*iii*) comfort in wearing and (*iv*) durability.

    7 The popular slogan says 'There is no substitute for wool.' Discuss this, stating whether you agree or not and giving your reasons.

(A.E.B.)

    8*a* Describe briefly how Crimplene is produced.

    b List the characteristics of the fabric.

    c State, giving reasons, the type of threads which should be used when sewing this fabric. (A.E.B.)

    9*a* Why is cotton such a popular textile fibre?

    b Name *six* different fabrics made from cotton and explain briefly the visible characteristics of each. (A.E.B.)

    10 List *four* natural fibres. Name a fabric which could be made from each, and say for what type of garments *two* of these fabrics could be used. Give reasons for your answers. (A.E.B.)

The following table shows suitable methods of working the seams, hems, fastenings, etc., on a selection of garments. These points should be noted:

1 The amounts quoted are average figures for 87–92 cm bust sizes.

2 The amounts shown are for knee-length garments for average height. Lengths should be adjusted for shorter or taller figures and changes in fashion lengths, e.g. if skirts are worn 5 cm above the knee, 5 cm can be deducted from lengths given for 140 cm

wide material and 10 cm (2×5 cm) from lengths given for 90 cm wide material.

3 Where more than one method is suggested under the same heading, they are alternatives and should not necessarily all be included on the same garment.

4 The methods suggested are not necessarily the *only* correct ones. On some garments and some materials different methods may be advisable for various reasons.

Garment	Suitable Materials	Amounts Required	Seams	Methods of Reducing Fullness	Hems	Fastenings	Decorative Processes	Other Processes
SKIRTS **Straight**	Tweed, woollen mixtures, gaberdine	0·8–1 m (140 cm wide)	Flat	Darts at waist Inverted or knife pleat at centre back	Raw edge neatened with crossway bind Slip hemmed	Zip fastener at side Hook and eyes, Jupefix, Velcro or buttons and buttonhole at waistband		Arrow head Setting on waistband
	Linen	1·6–2·2 m (90 cm wide)						
Slightly flared	Linen/polyester	As above	As above	As above	As above	As above		As above
Pleated	Worsted, fine tweeds, gaberdine, 55% + synthetic blends, linen/polyester	1·6–2·2 m (140 cm wide)	As above	Knife, box or inverted pleats	As above	As above		As above
	Linen	2·4–3·3 m (90 cm wide)						
Dirndl	Cottons, lawn, cotton/polyester blends	1·6–4·4 m (90 cm wide)	As above	Gathers at waist	Straight hem fixed with invisible hemming Machine edge-stitch raw edge and slip hem	As above	Ric-rac braid, coloured binding or embroidered ribbon in bands	Setting on waistband
Gored	Gaberdine, cottons, fine wools, linen, rayon	1·6–3·3 m according to width	As above		Neatened with crossway binding	As above		As above

Garment	Suitable Materials	Amounts Required	Seams	Methods of Reducing Fullness	Hems	Fastenings	Decorative Processes	Other Processes
Circular	Cottons, very fine wools, rayons	3·3–4·4 m (90 cm wide) 3·6–4·4 m (140 cm wide)	As above		Faced with crossway binding or a very narrow hem	As above		Setting on waistband Levelling hem after it has dropped
BLOUSES /TUNICS **Sleeveless**	Cottons, poplin, lawn, seersucker, nylon, rayon	1·2–1·4 m (90 cm wide)	French seams on sides and at shoulders	Gathers/tucks from shoulders Darts at waist if required Darts at underarm	Simple hem fixed with invisible hemming	Buttons and buttonholes down front opening Hook and worked bar under collar	Embroidery, Top-stitching Applique Pin-tucks Shadow work Faggoting Decorative stitching Frills Lace	Setting on collar Facing or binding armhole
Short-sleeved	As above Also fine wools	1·4–1·6 m (90 cm wide) 0·9 m (140 cm wide)	French seams on thin fabrics Flat seams on thicker ones Overlaid seams on yokes	As above	As above	As above	As above	Setting in sleeve Attaching cuffs Attaching collar
Long-sleeved	As above Also jersey	1·8–2·3 m (90 cm wide) 1·3–1·7 m (140 cm wide)	As above	As above Also gathers at wrist	As above	As above Button/ buttonhole on cuffs	As above	As above Working sleeve opening
DRESSES **Short-sleeved**	Cotton, rayons, woollens, linen, nylon, synthetic poplin, lawn	2·7–4·9 m (90 cm wide) 1·9–4·6 m (140 cm wide)	Flat seams Overlaid seams on midriffs	Gathers at waist, yokes or midriff Pleats in skirt Tucks in bodice Darts at waist and underarm	Work according to shape of skirt and type of material	Buttons/ buttonholes on front openings Buttons/loops on back neck opening Zip fasteners at front or back	Tucks Pleats Frills Lace	Working waist seam Finishing sleeve hems Attaching collar Setting in sleeve

	Fabric	Width	Seams	Fullness	Hems	Fastenings	Top-stitching	Finishing
Long sleeved	Cottons, rayons, woollens, linen, synthetics, jersey, corduroy	3·1-3·5 m (90 cm wide) 2·1-5 m (140 cm wide)	As above	As above	As above	As above Buttons/rouleau loops or press fasteners at wrist	As above Top-stitching	As above Wrist finish
LINGERIE Waist slip	Rayon, silk, cambric, nylon, jersey, lawn, tricel	1·6-2·4 m (90 cm wide)	French seams at side Flat seams (using selvedge edges) on frills	Gathers Darts Elastic at waist	Faced at waist Scalloped Shell-edged Net-edged Faggotted rouleau Frills	Small buttons and buttonholes at waist Lingerie zip (if waist is not elasticated)	Frills Lace Ribbons	Attaching waistband elastic Waist opening
Slip	As above	2·1-3·2 m (90 cm wide)	As above Overlaid seam for brassière top	As above	As above	Lingerie zip	As above Shadow work Net applique Embroidery	Attaching shoulder straps
NIGHT-WEAR Night-dresses	Lawn, brushed nylon, Viyella, jersey, rayon, cambric, silk / Winceyette	2·3-4·0 m (90 cm wide)	As above / Double stitched	Gathers Smocking / Gathers	Simple hem hemmed Frilled Shell-edged / Simple hem hemmed	Buttons/ buttonholes or rouleau loops / Buttons/ buttonholes	As above	Setting in sleeves / Attaching collar Sleeve finish Setting in sleeve
Pyjamas	Lawn, brushed nylon, Viyella, jersey, rayon, cambric, silk, Winceyette	3·6-4·1 m (90 cm wide)	Double stitched	Gathers Elastic at waist Darts	Simple hem hemmed	Buttons/ buttonholes		As above
Housecoats	Viyella, brushed nylon, fine wool, cotton (seersucker, cotton satin, etc) / Blanket cloth, fleece	3·7-5·5 m according to width	Flat	Pleats	Simple hem invisibly hemmed / Herringboned	Buttons and buttonholes/ rouleau loops Zip fastener	Frills Pipings Appliqué Lace	Attaching pockets Setting on collar Setting in sleeves Sleeve finish

GENERAL QUESTIONS

1 Write notes on *three* of the following:

a the different types of machine threads now available and their use.

b the different methods of transferring markings on to fabric, stating when each method is most suitable

c the equipment needed for embroidery

d the occasions when hand-sewing is preferable to machine-stitching. (C.U.B.)

2 Give detailed instructions with diagrams for the working of *four* of the following, stating when each would be used:

a tailor tacking

b slip basting

c slip hemming

d gathering stitch

e edge-stitching

f overcasting.

3 What is meant by 'press as you go along', and why is it so important?

Describe the pressing equipment needed for dressmaking, and the care necessary to keep it in good condition. What items could you make for yourself to help in pressing?

4 Explain, with the help of diagrams, the differences between

a a binding and a facing

b tucks and darts

c 'cross-cut' and 'bias'

d a panel and a gore

e plain and twill weave.

5 Explain as fully as possible:

a the difference in size of machine needles and their use

b the value of a thimble when sewing

c the differences between 40, 50 and tacking threads and their use

d the necessity for a large flat area for cutting out.

6 What do you understand by 'interfacing'? Name three different types and describe how you would make use of each, showing the fabric and the position in each case.

7 Show by description and illustration that you understand *four* of the following:

    a piping

    b selvedge

    c layering

    d slip stitching

    e rouleau

    f appliqué. (A.E.B.)

8 Describe briefly your own figure type.

Sketch, with comments, an outfit to emphasize your good points and minimize the weaker points. Give details of style, fabric, texture and colour. (C. & G.)

9 Discuss when and why a dressmaker shrinks material. (C. & G.)

10 What is the difference between lining and interlining? Mention two types of lining and two types of interlining which you have used. Give brief comments on each. (C. & G.)

MORE DIFFICULT QUESTIONS
(including some which require further research)

1 State points you would consider when designing garments to be made in any *three* of the following:

    a a checked fabric

    b a fabric with an irregular check

    c an all-wool fabric

    d a 100% terylene fabric. (C. & G.)

2 Discuss dress for schoolwear and its possible development. Illustrate your answer. (C. & G.)

3 How does a modern automatic sewing machine help the home dressmaker to produce garments speedily, efficiently and with a professional finish? (C. & G.)

4 What points must be considered when setting in a one-piece sleeve?

Why should the amount of ease on a sleeve-head differ when *a.* satin, *b.* fine wool and *c.* loosely-woven tweed are used?

5 Write about each of the following materials:

    a needlecord

    b gaberdine

    c bouclé

    d P.V.C.

    e double cloth. (C. & G.)

6 Suggest a bold and unusual type of decoration for:

a the sleeves of a teenager's dress

b the hemline of a girl's summer dress.

Explain briefly the method of working *one* type of decoration and state the materials required.   (C. & G.)

7 How are the following recognized?

a terylene lawn

b piqué

c denim

d grosgrain.   (C. & G.)

8 Suggest a suitable finish for *two* of the following:

a the edge of a chiffon frill

b the hem of a nightdress in brushed nylon

c the lower edge of a pair of slacks in stretch material.

Show the working of *one* of the finishes.   (C & G).

9 Show by sketches *four* ways of using striped material to achieve interest in cut. State the material you would use for each example.
                                                                      (C. & G.)

10 Illustrate *three* examples of decorative yet functional forms of fastening.   (C. & G.)

11 Describe bonded and non-woven fabrics and discuss their uses in fashion today.   (C. & G.)

12 Discuss some of the important changes in design and making up that have occurred because of present-day materials and equipment.
                                                                      (C. & G.)

13 Mention three processes which, although they may not be in use at the moment, you consider important for a dressmaker to understand. Give reasons.   (C. & G.)

14 Sketch and give brief notes about the use of smocking in *two* of the following:

a traditional English costume

b lingerie

c children's wear

d current fashion for teenagers.   (C. & G.)

15 What major changes have taken place in women's fashion over the last few years?   (C. & G.)

INDEX